PLAN YOUR FORTUNE

The Practical Guide to Regular Saving

PLAN YOUR FORTUNE

The Practical Guide to Regular Saving

Keith Taylor

The Mark Press
London and New York

First printed 1990
Reprinted 1990

The Mark Press
Mark House
39 Tollington Road
London N7 6PB
United Kingdom

British Library Cataloguing in Publication Data
Taylor, Keith, 1959–
Plan your fortune: the practical guide to regular saving.
1. Personal finance. Savings.
I. Title
339.43

ISBN 1-872928-00-5

Printed in Great Britain by Antony Rowe Ltd., Chippenham, Wilts.

Plan Your Fortune: The Practical Guide to Regular Saving has been written in order to provide comprehensive information concerning the subject matter covered. Both the author and the publisher have taken all reasonable care in the preparation of this book, but its accuracy cannot be warranted. The text, tables, examples and illustrations contained in this book do not constitute advice on making, changing or refraining from changing any particular investment. Readers who require expert advice on investment or related matters should seek the services of a competent professional adviser. For this reason, neither the author nor the publisher will be responsible for any loss arising from investments made, changed or left unchanged because of reliance placed on statements contained in this book.

Contents

Preface

The financial services industry has failed the small saver. As I see it, the major lending institutions encourage people to borrow money, in many cases beyond prudent and acceptable levels, particularly as far as mortgages are concerned. Students are offered considerable sums in loans, but this is rarely accompanied by sensible advice on money management. These institutions are very accessible to the public and, I believe, have an obligation to give sound, balanced financial advice. This is simply not possible with each organisation promoting its own in-house products such as insurance, pensions and unit trusts, often via poorly-trained staff who don't always understand the products they sell.

Similarly, insurance salesmen and 'financial consultants' have a lot to answer for. Less than 20 per cent of the population has adequate life insurance cover and the number of working people who retire comfortably well off is woefully small. Many in the insurance and pension industries regret these facts but how can matters be improved when the word 'insurance' has become almost a swear word, provoking an aggressive and hostile response from perhaps the majority of normally sane people? This is a sad reflection on an industry whose aim should be to provide its customers with the right amount of money in the right hands at the right time. The fact is, however, that most people do not seek out insurance – it has to be sold to them. How do insurance companies and intermediaries expect to promote the usefulness of their products with such a bad reputation and, also, in such a restrictive legislative environment?

The financial services industry has only itself to blame for the disastrous legislation known as the Financial

Services Act. The industry has failed to inform and guide the government in a positive and effective way to help it produce meaningful legislation which protects the public – the consumers of financial services. I find it inexcusable that the industry as a whole did not advise the government that simply signing client agreement letters (which describe a stockbroker's services and terms of business) provides no protection for clients against losing money, nor against their financial advisers giving bad advice. The sheer cost to everyone in the industry of complying with the Act has been enormous, and the small independent advisers have been particularly hard hit. Who pays for all this additional paper? Ultimately, of course, it is the small investor, through higher commissions and other management or service charges. This can hardly be in the consumers' interest, especially when you consider how little effective investor protection the Financial Services Act provides. The root of the problem is clearly education and surely the industry should understand and actively encourage this?

Since World War II, I believe that society has been increasingly conditioned to spend money. Demand for goods, whether essential or cosmetic, was initially promoted through press and cinema advertising. More recently, television has become a powerful influence on the way we spend our money, supported, in the last few years, by more readily available credit, making it even easier to buy goods and services. After so long being shown how to spend money, I, and some others, have begun to wonder if perhaps society has forgotten how to save – witness, for example, the dramatic drop in the personal sector savings' ratio in the last decade.

In recognition of this, the 1990 Budget Statement heralded the government's intention of encouraging a 'culture of thrift'. Although novel tax incentives will help towards this aim, the opportunities created will only be put to good use by the financially aware. After 45 years of conditioning, few people appreciate the personal economic and social benefits of saving and thrift and I believe that, here too, education is the only effective answer.

First, we need to educate our children at school, technical college and at university about financial planning and investment. This simply is not done at the moment. Secondly we should ensure that all staff giving advice to clients have a good background knowledge of a broad range of investments, and not just the ones in which they specialise. I think there should be a recognised, basic training course for the entire industry, attended by all staff who have dealings with the public. It is really the responsibility of government to police the industry effectively in order to weed out both the rogues and the incompetent, and the industry must be seen to be encouraging this by pressuring the government into providing better education on money matters. Until these things are achieved I see very little support or help forthcoming for our savers. The aim of this book is to offer them encouragement.

Keith Taylor
April, 1990

Acknowledgements

First, I would like to thank all those who have assisted in the production of this book and, in particular, Simon Perry of The Mark Press for his help and guidance.

There are also some key people who deserve special mention – Guy Hague for his valuable advice and for allowing me to use the production facilities at Zeralynx Print, along with Andy Glover in the Art Department and his assistant Katy Taylor. I would like to thank them all for the long hours and late nights they gave up to produce a very well-presented manuscript.

I am extremely grateful to Mum for slaving away at the computer all those hours to input the text and for being my secretary. Thanks also to Dad for some valuable suggestions and advice. My parents were a tower of strength to me while I was writing this book, providing the help and support to see me through a very difficult time. I dedicate the book to them.

Introduction

I have been an investor now for many years and I work in the financial services industry. I have travelled around the country a lot and have been appalled at people's attitude towards saving, and their ignorance on the subject. I have seen people tempted into parting with their hard-earned cash and speculating with it, either directly or indirectly, on the stockmarket. These were people fundamentally unsuited to such an investment and who could ill afford to lose any of their savings. They had been encouraged to speculate in order to accumulate and to invest without understanding and for all the wrong reasons, only to be disillusioned and poorer after the Crash of October 1987.

My aim with this book is to encourage savers. It shows that you do not have to speculate to accumulate and that you really can turn pennies into worthwhile sums of money through regular saving. Some people do make a lot of money from speculation, but for every one that succeeds there are so many that fail – and you rarely get to hear about these.

Good savers are made not born. Education is the key and the objective for this book is to provide a step-by-step guide explaining how to go about saving in a careful and methodical manner. Part I ('Your Task') sets out the basics of saving and financial planning and goes on to show how saving even the smallest amounts can be of enormous benefit to you and your family. Above all you will be encouraged to adopt the right attitude in order to become a successful saver. In Part II ('Your Choices') the range of products available to the regular saver is examined in detail. Discussion of each product is structured so that you will be able to decide how suitable it is for your own personal circumstances and needs. Finally, Part III ('How to Use Your Choices') concentrates on the inevitable changes in circumstances and objectives which we all experience periodically throughout our lives, and aims to help you ask the right questions at the right time in order to keep your finances on course for a wealthy future.

There are many excellent books on lump sum investment, but meaningful and practical advice to savers on how to accumulate these lump sums is very thin on the ground. This book contains such advice and I can only hope that it reaches the people who need it most. In any event, if you decide to take some of this advice I believe you will pay for the book many times over.

TAX EXEMPT SPECIAL SAVINGS ACCOUNTS

In the 1990 Budget, the Chancellor announced the introduction of a new savings scheme specifically designed to encourage the small saver. At the time of writing, the details of how it will work in practice are not known, but I think it is important in a book such as this to outline the broad framework of the new scheme.

From 1st January, 1991, anyone over 18 will be able to open a Tax Exempt Special Savings Account ('TESSA') with a bank or building society. The account will operate for five years and, provided savings are left intact for the full period, all interest earned will be tax free. Up to £9000 may be deposited over the five years, which translates into £150 per month as far as regular savers are concerned. The new scheme is surprisingly flexible – it will allow people to save on a regular basis or, if they have erratic earnings, irregularly. There will also be a facility permitting the withdrawal of interest, net of basic-rate tax, as it arises.

During the five-year period, investors will not be noticeably better off as a result of joining the scheme. The difference comes at the end of the term when the depositor receives a bonus representing the money which otherwise would have been paid in tax. This entitlement applies provided none of the capital has been withdrawn before the five years is up; if it has, this will lead to the cancellation of all tax advantages. Thus if the need arises, withdrawal of capital is possible within the five years (although at the expense of tax-free status), together with any accrued interest net of basic-rate tax. At the end of five years it will be possible to open a new TESSA and transfer up to £3000 into it in the first year.

Until we know the minimum investment and how competitive the returns will be when the TESSAs are in operation it is difficult to see how the accounts might suit non-taxpayers. For taxpayers, however, the advantages are clear.

PART I

YOUR TASK

1 The Key Message

The key message is that you do not have to be rich, or have privileged information or be earning a fortune in order to turn pennies into hundreds of pounds. So how is it done? *Plan Your Fortune* is a step-by-step guide to saving and the variety of methods of investing money on a regular basis – from just a few pennies to as much as you like.

But knowledge in itself may not always be enough. Many of us just refuse to believe that we can ever be better off unless a large slice of luck comes our way – for example, a rich uncle's legacy or a football pools win. This is simply not true. Everyone can become better off if they combine some knowledge with a new attitude to saving.

A CHANGE OF ATTITUDE

Saving has a dull and boring image nowadays and, at the same time, we've been encouraged to believe that it is always better to borrow money. Television and other media advertisements constantly show people borrowing to buy their dream car or the holiday of a lifetime. The friendly bank manager swells their bank balances by just the right amount and fortunately the borrowers in the adverts mysteriously appear to be able to pay back the money in the same casual way they received it – as if by waving a magic wand. The necessity of repaying, though, never receives the same emphasis as the desirability of borrowing.

Nowadays credit is so easy to obtain. We are constantly told that we can have what we want instantly if we borrow the money. Those who are easily tempted borrow too much and end up badly in debt. Often, the luxuries they once had are repossessed and they are still left with the burden of debt to repay. The sad thing is that the number of people getting into financial difficulty through borrowing has increased dramatically in recent years and this can cause serious family and social problems. The question to be considered must be: Is borrowing worth it?

Saving successfully on a regular basis often requires a change of attitude towards borrowing money as well as cultivating a positive attitude towards saving. This may be very difficult if you can only afford to save a few pence a week, but is the reason you can only afford to save such a small amount that you are borrowing too much – in other words that you have a negative attitude towards saving? If this is the case, becoming better off will require a more evenly balanced attitude towards both borrowing and saving.

2 Borrowing Versus Saving

BORROWING

As I have mentioned before, it is easy to borrow money. Having seen the new television set or the car of your dreams it is not difficult to go up to the salesman in the showroom, point to what you want and, as long as you can afford the monthly payments, to simply take the goods away. Surprisingly few people properly think through what they have let themselves in for when they borrow money like this. Let us consider the implications by looking at an actual example of buying a TV and video recorder on hire purchase (see Exhibit 2.1).

The first thing to note is the cash price of the two items. Beneath this, and adding considerably to the cost, is a service charge (i.e. for maintaining and repairing the goods) which has to be included under the terms of this particular agreement. A customer paying cash could

Exhibit 2.1 The cost of buying a television and video recorder under an HP agreement

Item	*Price (£)*
Television set	249.99
Video recorder	279.99
	529.98
Plus service charge	83.01
	612.99
Less initial cash payment	30.00
	582.99
Plus interest charges	233.49
Balance to pay	816.48
Monthly repayment over three years	22.68

choose whether to pay for this service facility or not. Next is the initial cash payment or deposit. Most agreements require a deposit or, at the very least, that something be traded in in lieu of a deposit. For agreements over a shorter period a larger deposit may be required.

Finally there are the interest charges, and in this particular case the annual percentage rate (or APR – the real interest charge, not just the nominal percentage) works out at around 26 per cent. This all adds up to 36 payments of £22.68 per month in addition to the £30 deposit.

It is worth setting out the realities of such an agreement:

1. The buyer is perfectly prepared to pay £846.48 for goods and services worth just £529.98. That is £316.50 over the top – more than the price of another TV or video. If you paid £800 for a second hand car and a reputable friend told you that in fact it was only worth £500 would you still feel as happy?
2. You may have to save for the deposit. How easy or difficult is that going to be?
3. Can you really afford to commit yourself to the monthly payments over that period of time? Will you have more or less financial commitments during the next three years?
4. Don't forget, the goods are not yours until you have finished paying for them. What happens if you have an unexpected large bill to pay, or you lose your job and cannot afford the payments? In this particular case the agreement says you would have to return the goods together with half the total amount payable under the agreement (i.e. £423.24). If you found yourself in this position after a few months, you would still have to pay money for goods you no longer have: if you had paid off half your agreement total or more, you would be left with nothing to show for it.
5. How much are these goods going to be worth once you have finished paying for them in three years time? The answer is very little – on a trade-in, around five

times your monthly payments (i.e. in this illustration, about £115).
6. The only advantage to this method of buying things is that you have the use of the goods before you finish paying for them.

SAVING

Let us look at the example in Exhibit 2.1 once again, but this time through the eyes of the saver.

One way of saving for the TV and video would be to save £22.68 per month (i.e. the same amount you would have to pay if you bought the goods under the hire purchase agreement). With this method you would have enough money to buy the goods after only 24 months, and don't forget you would have the choice whether or not to pay for the servicing. In this context, these are some of the advantages of saving:

1. You only need pay the asking price.
2. You may be able to negotiate a substantial discount for cash.
3. Credit agreements may not be available on all the goods in the shop. If you like something else for the same price or less, you can choose that instead if you have already saved the money.
4. Once you have paid for the goods they are yours, so you have something to sell if the need arises.
5. If, whilst saving for luxuries, you have an unexpected bill to pay you can always dig into these savings to get yourself out of a sticky situation.
6. There will be no need to worry if you can afford the payments this month – you will have paid for the goods.

So, saving for a purchase carries some major advantages. Essentially it provides choice and flexibility and none of the hassle of becoming tied up in a financial commitment you may not be able to keep.

This does not mean that borrowing is always bad. There is a place for sensible borrowing, but there are certain factors which should be examined before you buy now and pay later and, in my opinion, the most important of these is inflation.

INFLATION

One of the arguments put forward for buying now and paying later is that the goods you want this year will cost you more next year. This may well be true, but by how much? That is the question that has to be answered before you go ahead and borrow rather than save. To get the right answer we have to examine what effects inflation can have on the value of our money.

As can be seen from Exhibit 2.2, even with a modest inflation rate of 5 per cent the value of our money halves in roughly 14 years. At 15 per cent inflation the value of money halves in a frightening 5 years. This is why it does not pay to borrow money to purchase luxury items when inflation is low, but it would when inflation is very high. Think of it like this. If, in our hire purchase example, you expect that the goods are going to cost £846.48 or more in

Exhibit 2.2 The future value of £1000 in today's money (£s)

	Annual inflation rate				
Year	*5%*	*8%*	*10%*	*12%*	*15%*
1	952	926	909	893	870
2	907	857	826	797	756
3	864	794	751	712	658
4	823	735	683	636	572
5	784	681	621	567	497
6	746	630	564	507	432
8	677	540	466	404	327
10	614	463	386	322	247
15	481	315	239	183	123
20	377	215	149	103	61

three years time anyway (implying an inflation rate of around 16 per cent plus), you would be better off borrowing the money to buy them. If, on the other hand, you decide to save for the goods you may be earning some interest on your money, and this should also be taken into account. The inflation rate would then have to be higher again by as much as the net (i.e. after tax) return you receive on your money.

At the time of writing it is easily possible to secure a net return from a bank or building society which is slightly higher than the rate of inflation. Therefore it makes more sense than ever to save. A special feature of electrical goods is that their prices can behave in a peculiar way. When a new product is first marketed (e.g. video recorders) it is often very expensive. If, or when, the product becomes popular its price often drops dramatically. The same thing happened with calculators. So while you are saving you may find you are able to pay for an item earlier than you had expected.

BORROWING TO BUY A HOME

Incredible as it may seem, the same principles just discussed apply to house purchases. Assuming house price inflation is going to be low for the next three years, then it would benefit you to save £35,000 a year so that you could pay for your £100,000 house after the third year! Unfortunately, this is unrealistic for the vast majority of us. Instead, we will need to take advantage of conventional mortgage facilities and it will take at least 25 years to pay for our house.

Over such a long period of time it is impossible to predict house price inflation. There will be extremes of very rapid price rises over some periods, and possibly static or even falling prices over other periods. Since the Second World War house prices have risen at a faster rate than inflation. You could argue that in general your own home is a very good investment over the long term, and certainly for most people it is the biggest investment they make. As the country's population gets larger, and the demand for houses increases, the land on which they are built becomes more scarce. These factors will ensure that your home will remain a very good investment for as long as we can tell. Also, the government encourages us to borrow to buy a house by providing tax relief on mortgages up to £30,000. This makes the loan a cheap way of borrowing.

So it can pay to borrow money for a house. However, if you can afford to pay cash for your house it would be crazy to take out a mortgage, because you would be needlessly paying interest to the building society or bank. There is always a place for sensible borrowing as long as the payments can be easily afforded.

We live in a society in which we are encouraged to 'buy now and pay later' – but failing to think the options through and borrowing for all the wrong reasons can prove extremely expensive. It's important to recognise the problems and pitfalls, learn from mistakes and, as a result, begin the process of becoming substantially better off. The correct attitude is the key to success.

3 The Essentials of Saving

Saving is not simple. It is not easy to explain how to save, and it is one of the most difficult things to put into practice successfully. If saving was simple we would all be retiring owning our own house, with few financial commitments, and with enough money to live comfortably. These objectives are never accomplished by the majority of people because successful saving is hard to achieve.

I believe that the reality for most people is that it is easier to spend a pound than to save a penny, and there are various reasons why this is so:

1. Most people have a very limited income and out of this we all have to live somewhere, eat, keep warm and clothe ourselves. We might then have to support a family. After all that has been taken out of the pay packet, there may not be very much left to save.
2. Inflation makes life difficult for everyone if it gets out of hand. Prices rise but incomes lag behind, thereby forcing people to dig into their reserves.
3. Then there is temptation. It is so tempting to splash out on an extravagant holiday, a new car or the latest compact disc player, especially if the money to pay for them can be easily borrowed.
4. Attitude. Again this word crops up, but it is one of the key factors in unlocking the secrets of successful saving. Many people cannot be bothered to save and cannot see any reason for doing so. There is also a whole army of bewildered people who would like to save, probably very small sums of money, but do not know how to go about it. They would feel embarrassed to ask their bank or building society and neither would they go to a financial consultant for advice.

They would be scared of being pressured into buying something they did not want or scared of being told, politely, to go away because they do not have enough money.

Help is at hand for these would-be savers in the following pages.

REASONS FOR SAVING

Saving is the process of putting money aside so that it is available in the future. There are a wide variety of reasons for saving ranging from the important desire to have an emergency fund, to education and retirement planning. Whatever the reasons, they normally fall into three basic categories, as set out in Exhibit 3.1.

The two most important categories are the short- and long-term. First, for the short term everyone should aim to have an emergency fund to cope with the unexpected (e.g. a major repair on the car, or possible unemployment). An ideal amount to have immediately available as an emergency fund might be, say, three months' wages. This is the sort of target you should aim for.

The long-term category is extremely important and covers retirement and life insurance. Everybody should aim to retire comfortably off, and after a long life of toiling, it is only right that people should enjoy the fruits of their labour in retirement. Unfortunately many people still rely solely on the state pension which, for 1990–91, is £46.90 per week for a single person and £75.10 per week for a

Exhibit 3.1 The three categories of saving

Category	*Period*	*Examples*
Short-term	0–5 years	Emergency fund, car, holidays
Medium-term	5–15 years	Life insurance, education, house deposit
Long-term	15+ years	Retirement, life insurance

married couple. This is a very small sum to live on and, even if these people do have some savings, they risk running out of money before they die.

It is also important to consider life insurance, especially if you have a family. If the breadwinner should unexpectedly die, it is not fair that the remaining family should have to cope with extreme financial hardship as well as bereavement. Both these problems of living too long or dying too soon can be solved by regular saving through the right financial products. Unfortunately many people fail to recognise and face up to these problems until it is too late.

To sum up, if you do have any spare money left over from your income which you could afford to save on a regular basis, try and split it up into at least two categories. First, a fund for emergencies and second, no matter how young you are, something for your retirement. Then you can save for the luxuries in life.

4 Financial Planning

Now that we've discussed some of the benefits of saving we can begin working on turning pennies into sizeable sums of money.

Expecting your fairy godmother to wave her wand and make you rich is unfortunately not an option, but financial planning is. Worthwhile financial planning has to be both specific and realistic. You must have a reason for saving in order to give yourself the necessary motivation – set specific targets or goals that you know you have a good chance of achieving. Targets can range from quite simple, short-term aims (such as saving for a new stereo system or a holiday) to more complex medium- and long-term objectives (like buying a house or planning for retirement). Taking the short-term category as an example, for a young person a new stereo system may be the target; the prize for saving is the thrill of going to the shop and buying it with cash, plus the satisfaction of having achieved the planned objective. As we get older and our circumstances change, as well as short-term goals we tend to establish more long-term targets. Where people go wrong is that they don't develop the theme in the above example and apply it to their more sophisticated needs as their life-style develops.

Everyone needs to plan for their own financial future, no matter how poor or wealthy they may be. Financial planning is a way of setting out on paper exactly what you want to achieve and how you intend to achieve it. Regard it as your own financial map, drawn for yourself and by yourself, which works in the same way as a road map. First of all you need to discover where you are on the map and then identify where you want to go. The final stage is to find the route between A and B which best suits your needs. You can liken this stage to travelling from London to Paris – there are many routes you can take and many forms of transport you can use to get there. If you ask different people how they would do it you might get many different and interesting answers, but they could all be correct.

Your starting point is your current financial position. This will change when you change job, get married or have children, or when your children leave home or you retire, so it is important to re-assess your situation regularly. It is necessary to review your finances in detail to provide all the information required to produce a clear financial map. You will then be in a position to choose your financial targets and to pick out the routes available for achieving them. For this you may need some help.

WHERE ARE YOU NOW?

As with any map, you need the correct coordinates to find out exactly where you are. The two coordinates on your financial map are your assets, or what you are worth, and your liabilities, or what you spend or owe.

ASSETS

What are you really worth? The first thing that springs to mind is your income. How much are you earning, how much tax are you paying and are you paying too much? Can you think of any ways you can increase your income? Are you claiming all the benefits to which you are entitled? Most people judge what they are worth solely in terms of income, which only tells half the story. Don't forget that, just like a business, you need to know what you would be worth if you sold up tomorrow. For example, if you are buying your home, what is it worth now compared to what you paid for it? Maybe you have other assets. What savings do you have and do you have a bank or building society account? If you get paid some interest you will have some unearned income. Write down how much interest you receive no matter how small, as every penny counts. Other assets may include life insurance policies. If you have any, write down how many you have and what they are worth. Many people nowadays own unit trusts or possibly a few shares. Make a list and work out the dividends you receive from them. If you have only a small amount of such investments, are you making the maximum use of the income they produce? I have seen announcements from British Gas, saying that many small shareholders fail to cash their dividend cheques; similarly, many owners of premium bonds fail to collect their prizes because they forget to tell the Bonds and Stock Office their new address. It is incredible how many people turn away money that is rightfully theirs!

You now have a clearer idea of what you are worth and what assets you have which is the plus side, so now you have to consider your costs or outgoings.

OUTGOINGS

What are your own and your family's running costs? Start by adding up all your monthly standing orders and direct debits. Other bills may include rates, electricity, heating, food, clothes, car, holidays, Christmas, leisure, insurance and so on. Notice I have included Christmas! It comes around every year and yet very few people bother to budget for it. In the same way you must consciously budget for leisure activities – the occasional nice meal or a short break – so put something aside for these. Everyone will have a different list of expenses, but when you are calculating them it is better to overestimate costs in case you overlook something. With all your expenses try, if possible, to pay your bills on a regular and frequent basis (e.g. by monthly standing order or direct debit), or failing that, make a habit of putting money aside each month to cover regular bills.

I have included a budget planner checklist (Exhibit 4.1) which you may find helpful to fill in. You should then be able to see what you are spending on everyday living and on other regular outgoings. If you see that you are clearly spending too much in any particular area, you must cut

Exhibit 4.1 Plan your budget

A MONTHLY UTILITIES		
Electricity		
Water		
Telephone		
Gas/heating		
MONTHLY TOTAL		
B PERSONAL ALLOWANCES AND RECREATION		
Allowances for each family member (pocket money, hairdresser,tobacco, alcohol, etc. List as appropriate.)		
Family recreation (sport, club memberships, hobbies, etc.)		
MONTHLY TOTAL		
C OTHER EXPENSES (show annual amount)		
Insurance		
Accident		
Building		
House contents		
Life		
Vehicles		
Local taxes		
Medical (medicines, doctor, dentist, etc.)		
Education (uniforms, books, tuition, etc.)		
Licences (vehicles, television, other)		
Maintenance		
Home and furnishings		
Vehicles		
Gifts (Christmas, birthdays, etc.)		
Travel and holidays		
Other		
ANNUAL TOTAL		
MONTHLY TOTAL (divide total by 12)		

Exhibit 4.1 Plan your budget (contd.)

BUDGET PLANNER		
MONTHLY LIVING EXPENSES		
Food		
Housing		
Mortgage		
Rent		
Mortgage protection policy		
Mortgage endowment policy		
Household incidentals		
(eg laundry, newspapers)		
Utilities (total from box 'A' on previous page)		
Transport		
Petrol		
Bus/train fares		
Parking		
Other living expenses		
(child care, household		
help, alimony, etc.)		
Allowances (total from box 'B' on previous page)		
Other expenses (total from box 'C')		
TOTAL MONTHLY LIVING EXPENSES		1
MONTHLY SAVINGS		
Emergency fund		
Pension		
Savings plans		
Other savings		
TOTAL MONTHLY SAVINGS		2
MONTHLY CREDIT PAYMENTS		
Hire purchase		
Credit cards		
Store credit		
Overdraft		
Other loans		
TOTAL MONTHLY CREDIT PAYMENTS		3
TOTAL MONTHLY BUDGET (add lines 1, 2 and 3)		

back immediately. This may mean some difficult decisions but it is important to be resolute and determined. You must decide what your priorities are and, if you find you are struggling to make ends meet, you can then immediately cut back on less important expenses. Hopefully saving will already be a priority expense for which you are currently budgeting and with any luck you will also have a bit of a surplus left over. Even if your budget doesn't balance, there are still ways in which it is possible to save money which I will discuss later on. Balancing your budget is vital because only then can you begin to make money.

WHERE ARE YOU GOING?

Now that you have put all the coordinates on your financial map, you can see exactly what your financial position is. First check that your budget is balanced and adjust your spending if necessary. Then work out how much you can spend after your regular commitments and split it into two – the short-term and long-term funds.

Next, start to decide on your financial goals by trying to look forward into the future. For instance, have you made any plans for your retirement – if not, would you be satisfied with living on just the state pension? Probably not. Therefore your long-term aims might include being able to retire comfortably well off, which is a realistic goal if you start planning for it early enough. Here are a few additional examples of financial targets. Short-term goals might include:

1. Establishing an emergency fund;
2. Travel;
3. A new car;
4. Furnishings;
5. Clothes;
6. Hobbies;
7. Sports equipment;
8. Other luxuries.

Longer-term objectives might include:

1. Building up capital;
2. Providing for your children's education;
3. Other financial help for the children;
4. Buying a property;
5. Financial security;
6. Comfortable retirement.

You may have a few more goals to add to these lists, but in any case mark the ones that are important to you. From the shortlists, choose one or more short-term goals and put your long-term aims into priority order. Now, to what extent and how quickly you achieve these goals depends on your income and assets. Part II of this book examines the major products available to help you; for your part, you must provide the right attitude and determination to achieve the goals you have set.

You should now have a clear idea of the sort of financial targets you want to aim at and be in a position to start choosing which route to take in order to achieve them. You may decide to choose your own course of action or seek further advice, but whatever you decide to do you should now be asking the right questions to enable you to build up a financial plan. If you review the plan regularly you will be sure to get the best out of your resources.

PART II

YOUR CHOICES

5 The Range of Choices

In this part of the book I have set out to explain and analyse the range of products available to the regular saver. There are other financial products on offer but I have attempted to stick to those which, in my opinion, can best be used by the small saver on a regular basis.

Each chapter begins by examining products with a very low initial investment and, proceeding through the chapter, the minimum investment level gradually climbs. The earlier chapters in the section deal with relatively unsophisticated and short-term products, while the later chapters become slightly more technical, and discuss predominantly longer-term investments. You may well be thinking that the longer-term products will be beyond your financial reach but you will be surprised at how little your minimum monthly investment needs to be to qualify.

Imagine this part of the book as a shop window or a supermarket, stacked full of financial products. Many people go through their entire lives without encountering such a shop and therefore have never had the opportunity to look in or browse around the shelves. If you walk round any supermarket you will find different people filling up their shopping baskets with different things to suit their needs and circumstances. With an investment shop you also need to pick an appropriate product to fit your own particular situation – making the wrong choices can cost money.

EMERGENCY FUNDS THROUGH TO PENSION PLANNING

In Part I we discussed the need to build up an emergency fund to provide for unexpected bills. For this objective, you should pick a product which lets you get at your money very quickly. The least appropriate investment for this purpose is a pension plan, because you have no access to your money until your retirement. The most appropriate products are provided by banks and building societies and they are described in the early chapters of this section. You need money to be readily available and therefore you must not choose an account which requires you to give a long period of notice before a withdrawal. The final step is to compare accounts to find out which one gives the most favourable return on your money. With such accounts the return will, of course, fluctuate in line with national interest rates.

The early chapters in Part II therefore deal with the types of products that people can use throughout their lives – they are short-term investment vehicles which are very flexible and carry little or no risk of losing any of your original investment. We then discuss National Savings, looking at some products that actually guarantee a specific return on your money. All of them, without exception, guarantee that your original investment is completely safe. If you prefer such products, you will have to sacrifice flexibility (relating to such matters as the minimum initial investment and notice of withdrawals). There are investments for the short and medium term and, in general, the longer the term of the investment the less flexible the product is. Unlike banks and building societies, National Savings is able to offer products with more advantageous returns to non-taxpayers and which are, therefore, particularly appropriate for pensioners or children. It also offers products which higher-rate taxpayers may find very suitable; provided they are prepared to tie their money up for a set period they will qualify for a guaranteed return. There are also some insurance products which guarantee a return, but the investor will have to wait longer to secure this – normally at least 10 years.

Insurance products and the other choices from Chapter Nine onwards are ideally suited to the long-term investor. These investments carry the risk of providing a very poor return if a plan is cashed in within the first few years. In return for the length of time over which you must hold the investment, and for the additional risk involved, the rewards are usually substantially better than for the choices discussed earlier in Part II. Many of the insurance products are ideally suited to married couples and families, where an element of protection in a savings plan is desirable. If, however, you are young and able to accept a higher-risk investment over the short term, and you simply do not need life insurance protection, then a unit or investment trust plan would suit you best. There is no point in paying for life insurance if you do not need it. Higher-rate taxpayers will also find insurance products very useful, but when they get older or their health is failing, insurance premiums may become expensive and, as a savings medium, a personal equity plan (or 'PEP') may suit their rather more risky investment strategy.

To sum up, there are investment products to suit everybody. Short-term, guaranteed, medium- and long-term investments are all available, and there are even products which aim to solve a particular problem, such as pensions. There are also investments for those prepared to take a risk in the short term in return for possibly much higher returns in the long term. There is bound to be something suitable for you, but you must make sure that it is appropriate otherwise it might result in you losing money rather than the reverse.

Before embarking on a detailed examination of the products provided by the financial institutions which are suitable for regular savers, let's look at the most obvious starting point – saving cash.

CASH

As I mentioned earlier, saving is the process of putting surplus money aside so that it is available in the future. So what could be more readily available than coins and notes themselves? As children, most of us have been introduced to saving in this way, by simply putting coins in our money box or piggy bank. As adults, many people regard this as a childish way of saving and dismiss it out of hand. However there are still many old people who keep their life savings in a drawer or under a mattress.

Instead of dismissing this method of saving as childish, we should first examine it on its merits. For a start it is a way of saving that even the poorest people can put into practice. In order to be successful though, you need to save regularly. First, choose a container – which could range from a big pickling jar to a proper piggy bank or cash tin – and aim to fill it up. Even an empty one-pound jam jar can hold over £10 in 5p, 2p and 1p coins. Next, choose the coins that you are going to save. You may, like me, dislike the 20p and 1p coins because they are too awkward to handle and are easily dropped or lost in pockets and purses. Every night before you go to bed, make a habit of looking through your change and popping them in your container instead of losing them. You will be surprised how quickly it starts to fill up, and amazed how much you have saved when your container is full. To encourage yourself further, why not save for a specific reason and spend the money on Christmas presents, for instance, or on a good night out. The point is that you choose your method, make a habit of it and stick to the routine regularly. This may be a very basic method of regular saving, but it can work extremely well for everybody and can also be surprisingly rewarding.

Advantages

1. The simplest method of saving.
2. Suitable even for the very poor.
3. Makes good use of change which is otherwise wasted or lost.
4. Instant access to your money.
5. A good way to introduce children to saving.
6. No tax to pay.

Disadvantages

1. Easily stolen.

2. Tempting to raid in order to buy small items.
3. No interest is received.
4. Inflation erodes the value of the money.
5. Time-consuming to count.

6 Bank Accounts

TAXATION TREATMENT

With just a few exceptions both bank and building society interest is paid net of basic-rate income tax to the investor. The institution pays a composite rate of tax ('CRT') to the Inland Revenue which, because it takes into account the fact that some customers are non-taxpayers, is below the basic rate of tax. It is important to note that non-taxpayers cannot reclaim the tax paid. Basic-rate taxpayers, whilst still having to declare the interest received to the Inland Revenue, are deemed to have paid basic-rate tax on the interest they receive. Higher-rate taxpayers may be liable to pay additional tax.

The situation described above will not last for very much longer because, in the 1990 Budget, it was proposed to abolish CRT with effect from 6th April, 1991. From this date, basic-rate taxpayers will receive their interest after the deduction of basic-rate tax, not CRT. A system will be devised whereby non-taxpayers will be able to receive interest without the deduction of tax; however, if they do receive interest net of basic-rate tax, they will be able to reclaim the tax paid. Higher-rate taxpayers will still be liable to pay additional tax as before. The abolition of CRT means that many non-taxpaying savers will no longer have to endure a stiff tax penalty for investing in banks and building societies. Thus, when reading the chapters on bank and building society accounts for regular savers it is important to remember that although non-taxpayers may lose out at present, things will change significantly after April 1991.

CURRENT ACCOUNTS

It may seem a bit odd to include current accounts in a book concerned with regular savings and investment – however, they can play a very important role. There are few people nowadays who do not have such an account and so it is important to make the best use of it.

It is quite simple to open a current account with any of the big high-street clearing banks. All you do is fill in an application form, possibly provide a reference, and open the account with a small deposit of a few pounds. In due course you will receive a cheque book, paying-in book and a cheque guarantee card which you should insist on having as it guarantees that your bank will honour cheques up to a certain amount (usually £50).

The current account has some major features that the regular saver can make good use of. First you have the ability to write cheques, which is a safe and simple way of paying bills and drawing cash. A cheque is basically a signed instruction to your bank to pay another person or business. You can keep track of what you spend by filling in all the details on your cheque counterfoils. This is an important facility in helping you to budget successfully. All the big four banks offer to send you a monthly statement which is a complete record of what money has gone into and out of your account. It is important that you check this statement against your cheque counterfoils so that you can keep a close eye on your financial situation. These two current account features make budgeting very simple and straightforward.

Current accounts also have the facility to pay regular bills without the need to remember to write and send cheques. This can be achieved either by direct debits or standing orders. Direct debits are paid following requests to your bank made by the organisation which you are paying. The amounts may vary but you do not have to give new instructions. The organisation you are paying will give you a form to complete which you return to them and they in turn forward to your bank. This is an excellent way for a regular investor to pay insurance premiums which may well vary. A standing order, on the other hand, is paid on your instructions and you have to send the bank new instructions each time the amount of the payment alters. If you find that you have a little spare cash left over in your account each month, you can use a standing order to transfer it into a savings account to earn some interest on the money. You will find that this is a very easy and convenient way of regularly building up your emergency cash fund. It is also an excellent method of putting aside regular amounts to pay for annual bills such as car tax or the TV licence.

You may receive other facilities with your current account such as a cashpoint card, which allows you to withdraw cash from a dispenser at any time.

OVERDRAFTS

One of the most important (and unique) features of a current account is that you can have access to more money than you actually possess as long as you seek your bank manager's permission. This takes the form of an overdraft, which is fixed at a set limit depending on your circumstances. An overdraft can be particularly valuable if you are suddenly presented with an unexpected bill but, in general, it is an uneconomical way of borrowing and should not be used, for example, for buying luxuries.

The fact is that it can be very expensive to go into the red with a current account because most banks offer free accounts to all those who stay in credit but charge heavily if your balance goes overdrawn. Typically, you can expect bank charges of 30p for each cheque, direct debit, standing order or cashpoint withdrawal you make in the charging period (usually three months) during which you go overdrawn. On top of this there is a quarterly account maintenance charge of about £12, plus the interest on the money you borrow, which of course varies from time to time. If, however, you maintain an average balance of £500 or more during the month you go overdrawn, you will not pay any charges. These charges are fairly typical, but there is some variation between the banks: Lloyds, for example, has a monthly charging period, not quarterly, with slightly different charges.

So current accounts offer very useful facilities which the saver can make good use of. The statements can form a basis for careful budgeting, and sensible use of standing orders can help you save conveniently and regularly. If you mismanage your account, however, the charges incurred can be considerable.

Advantages

1. Instant access to your money.
2. Money is safe. Cheques are a good way of sending money through the post.
3. Access to more money than you possess.
4. Current account statements help you to budget accurately and successfully.
5. Standing orders provide a convenient way of saving money.
6. No tax to pay.

Disadvantages

1. Not suitable for those who are paid in cash and pay all their bills in cash.
2. Very expensive to run if you go overdrawn.
3. Usually no interest is received.
4. Inflation erodes the value of your money.
5. Not recommended as a vehicle for saving in itself.

INTEREST RATES

Before going on to discuss bank and other investments that pay interest, I think this may be a good point at which to consider how interest rates are quoted and calculated.

It is possible for two different investment accounts to quote the same nominal interest rate and yet still pay different amounts of interest. This is usually due to the different ways in which interest is paid and, in order to compare the two investments, a true rate is quoted which takes into account the different payment methods. This

Exhibit 6.1 A nominal interest rate of 10 per cent per annum, paid quarterly

Period	*Opening balance (£)*	*Interest earned (£)*	*Closing balance (£)*
Quarter one	100.00	2.50	102.50
Quarter two	102.50	2.56	105.06
Quarter three	105.06	2.62	107.68
Quarter four	107.68	2.69	110.37

true rate is called the annual percentage rate or 'APR'. Consider, for example, a nominal interest rate of 10 per cent per annum (see Exhibit 6.1). If an account pays interest four times a year, or quarterly, the APR will be 10.37 per cent because, if this interest is left in the account, it also will earn interest.

Therefore, when you are comparing rates of interest beware. Always look at the APR figure which provides the true return and ensures you are comparing like with like.

INTEREST-BEARING CURRENT ACCOUNTS

These are a relatively recent innovation and it was not until 1989 that all the major banks began offering such a product in response to accounts already available from some building societies. Interest is paid on all credit balances. Some banks have two tiers of interest rates: usually a lower rate on balances below £500, and a higher rate on balances above that figure. You can expect the interest rate to be close to that paid on a bank deposit account.

Interest-bearing current accounts offer the same facilities as conventional current accounts, and therefore you will usually have to pay interest on any overdraft. One development, however, is that the accounts do not impose transaction charges if you go into the red, but instead charge a monthly or quarterly fee. These fees vary enormously from bank to bank. You may also find that some banks allow you to go up to £250 overdrawn before they charge interest on your overdraft.

Now that these current accounts are finally available from the major banks, it will probably not be too long before they replace the traditional current account. The interest received is not spectacular and is unlikely to give a return in excess of inflation, but it does at least mean that your money is earning interest every day you are not using it. So if you are particularly careful with your money this could also be a good place to keep some of your emergency fund, although psychologically there is a lot to be said for keeping this fund in an account which is separate from the one you use for day-to-day transactions.

Advantages

1. All the features of the traditional current account with the additional advantage of interest added to accounts in credit.
2. Can be used as an account in which to build up an emergency fund.

Disadvantages

1. As for traditional current accounts, but interest received reduces the effect of inflation on savings.

DEPOSIT ACCOUNTS

All the major banks offer deposit accounts, where money can be withdrawn at seven days notice without loss of interest, or on demand with loss of seven days interest on the amount you withdraw. The deposit account is probably the simplest savings account the banks offer. You can usually open an account with as little as £1 and add to it whenever you like. There are no minimum or maximum amounts after the initial deposit has been made. Usually the interest earned is added every six months, but the interest rate is often much lower than on other comparable accounts. You will normally be given a paying-in book to help you keep a record of your deposits, together with an annual statement.

Advantages

1. Once an account is open you can invest any amount at any time without entering into a regular commitment. Very flexible.
2. A good home for an emergency fund.
3. Easy access to your money.
4. Interest is paid on your money, usually half-yearly.
5. Ideal account to use in conjunction with your current account.

Disadvantages

1. Interest paid is often lower than the rate of inflation, so you rarely secure a real return on your money.
2. Seven days notice is needed to withdraw money without loss of interest.
3. Not suitable for non-taxpayers because tax cannot be reclaimed.

CHILDREN'S ACCOUNTS

All the banks have their own versions of these accounts which are basically deposit accounts with free gifts to encourage children to invest. The idea is to make it just as interesting and rewarding to save as it is to spend. A popular gift is an account-opening pack which might include an account record book, a paying-in book and space to store regular statements. Some banks also produce a magazine.

The interest on these children's accounts is normally a little higher than on an ordinary deposit account. You can obtain your money immediately but just like an ordinary deposit account you will normally lose seven days interest on the money withdrawn if you do not give seven days notice. Conditions and interest rates vary considerably from bank to bank.

Advantages

1. Encourages children to take an interest in saving money.
2. The interest rate is often higher than for a deposit account.
3. There is a better possibility of obtaining a real rate of return on your money in times of very low inflation.
4. It is almost worth opening an account for the free gifts alone.

Disadvantages

1. Not tax efficient for non-taxpayers because tax cannot be reclaimed. Most children are non-taxpayers and a better return can be obtained elsewhere.

MONTHLY SAVINGS ACCOUNTS

These accounts are particularly attractive to the small regular saver because the interest paid is normally substantially better than on ordinary deposit accounts – sometimes two per cent net above the deposit rate. Monthly savings accounts, in my opinion, should be much more popular than they are because they are ideal for achieving many of our short- to medium-term goals discussed in Part I. Their beauty is that you do not need a large lump sum to obtain a more advantageous interest rate. As little as £10 per month for a sustained period will secure the preferential rate.

The way to use a monthly savings account is to decide how much you can easily afford to save regularly. Ideally you should aim to reach a specific target – for instance, the cost of a holiday. Again the most convenient way of paying into the account is by standing order from a current account to ensure that you do not miss any regular payments. Interest is then paid to you at the end of each saving period which could be one year or, in some cases, every six months. Usually at the end of a savings period you can change the amount you want to save in the next period. Many schemes allow you to pay in an additional sum each month or allow you to miss one monthly payment in a savings period without penalty. Finally you are permitted to make one withdrawal without notice during any savings period. So there is some flexibility in these accounts making it easier for people to benefit from higher interest rates.

Advantages

1. Better interest paid than on deposit accounts.
2. No need for large capital sums to obtain the higher interest.
3. A relatively flexible way of saving regularly whilst obtaining a better return on your money.
4. A good method of saving for short- to medium-term goals.
5. The account encourages people to make a habit of saving regularly and therefore more effectively.

Disadvantages

1. It is possible to obtain better returns elsewhere, but usually at the expense of some flexibility.
2. A commitment has to be made to save regularly.
3. Those with less than £10 a month to save are usually not catered for.
4. Once your account has reached £1000 or more you would do better to transfer the money elsewhere to obtain a better return.
5. Tax on interest paid cannot be reclaimed by non-taxpayers.
6. If the savings are connected with a planned mortgage application then a mortgage savings account should be used instead.

MORTGAGE SAVINGS ACCOUNTS

These accounts are designed for the specific purpose of saving towards obtaining a mortgage. In times of readily available credit the accounts tend to be unnecessary and unpopular and, in recent years, have become something of an 'endangered species'. Again you receive an attractive rate of interest and, at the end of the period, you are guaranteed a mortgage. This is a very useful way of obtaining a mortgage at a set date when there is a mortgage queue. Account terms vary enormously between institutions, but a regular sum must be saved every month for a defined period. The minimum varies from as little as £10 up to £50 per month and it is important to shop around for the most attractive deal.

Advantages

1. A guarantee of a mortgage at the end of the period.
2. A good rate of interest paid.

Disadvantages

1. A very specialised product (specifically for mortgage savers) more suited to the larger, regular saver.
2. Terms and conditions vary considerably from bank to bank.

HIGHER-RATE DEPOSIT ACCOUNTS

Higher-rate deposit accounts are offered under different names by the various institutions. In order to open one you will need to deposit a lump sum, from as little as £500 but usually £1000. This minimum balance must be maintained on your account if you are to benefit from the higher interest paid. The interest levels increase as your account balance reaches higher levels. For instance with Lloyds Bank the interest bands are £1000, £5000, £10,000 and £50,000. Most of the other banks have a band at £10,000 but their other levels vary quite a lot. The other feature of these accounts is instant access to your money with no interest penalty for immediate withdrawals.

These accounts can only be of use to the regular investor who has already saved a reasonable emergency fund. Just a note of caution here – before you decide to switch, make sure the rate of interest you receive on the higher-rate deposit account is higher than on your monthly savings account. The reason is that you may need to make an initial deposit of £5000 to secure this better rate. This, of course, varies from bank to bank, so do shop around. Once you have achieved the minimum balance, you will have the flexibility to deposit any additional sum you wish, but you may prefer to retain the regular saving discipline by adding a set amount of money to the account each month by standing order.

Advantages

1. At the higher bands, better interest rates can be obtained with these accounts than the others previously mentioned.
2. In times of low inflation you are likely to achieve a real return on your money.
3. Once you have deposited the minimum balance, these accounts are very flexible.
4. Higher bands bring higher interest.
5. Very competitive interest rates which are often difficult to beat.

Disadvantages

1. You may need quite a sizeable sum in order to open this account and receive the interest premium over regular savings accounts.
2. The account balance must not fall below the minimum requirement.
3. Only useful to regular savers who already have a reasonable emergency fund.
4. Under normal circumstances interest is paid net, and tax cannot be reclaimed by the non-taxpayer.

HIGH-INTEREST CHEQUE ACCOUNTS

In order to open one of these accounts, similar conditions normally apply as for the higher-rate deposit accounts. The similarity starts with the fact that most institutions insist on a minimum deposit, commonly £2000–£2500. This minimum balance must always be maintained and as before, you may find that as your account reaches a certain level you qualify for a higher interest band. The attractiveness of these accounts is the cheque book and the flexibility that it brings. You have instant access to your money without loss of interest if notice isn't given, but most of these cheque accounts insist on a minimum withdrawal, normally £200–£250. Some accounts do not impose any charges but, instead, offer lower rates of interest: more often, you will be allowed one or two free withdrawals each month, beyond which you will pay a set charge for each transaction. All these conditions vary considerably and it is important to compare the terms offered by each of the banks in order to decide which product suits you best. You will normally receive a cheque guarantee card and regular statements and direct debit and standing order facilities are usually available. Interest is credited quarterly or monthly.

As with the higher-rate deposit accounts, these cheque book accounts have a limited appeal for the regular saver because of the sizeable lump sum normally required to open an account. However, the added flexibility of a cheque book may appeal to you and you may be able to find an account that requires a minimal deposit.

There is a cheque book account offered by Western Trust and Savings which does not fit into the category of just current account or high-interest account – it has qualities of both. It is called 'current account plus' and offers the normal features of a current account, including an overdraft facility (not provided with high-interest cheque accounts), and it also pays interest quarterly on balances in excess of £500 with the interest rate increasing as your account reaches bands at £1000, £5000 and £10,000.

Advantages

1. As with higher-rate deposit accounts.
2. Added flexibility of a cheque book.

Disadvantages

1. As with higher-rate deposit accounts.

2. Beware of the small print when opening such accounts as you may find that you will have to pay sizeable charges for withdrawals.
3. These accounts have a very limited appeal to most regular investors and although they may be flexible enough, you will need to carefully consider your own circumstances before deciding such an account is suitable.

SUMMARY

Compared to other financial institutions, banks offer a tremendous range of services and the regular saver is well catered for because the accounts we have considered offer a good home for emergency money and are ideal for achieving short-term goals.

All the major banks are easily accessible through local branch networks so it is easy to open and run a savings account. Your money is safe and your capital will be repaid in full. Any interest you receive will be paid regularly, normally net of basic-rate tax which suits taxpayers very well, and your savings are not assessed for capital gains tax. In the unlikely event of your bank getting into financial difficulties, the Deposit Protection Board guarantees that small investors (up to £10,000) will recover 75 per cent of their money.

Regular savings accounts provided by the banks do not offer a guaranteed return. Interest rates fluctuate and, over the long term, rarely exceed inflation.

Basic-rate tax is deducted and cannot be reclaimed and therefore non-taxpayers may well find better returns elsewhere. There are no prospects for capital growth on your original capital which makes bank account investments unattractive for medium- to long-term savings and investment. The major risk for the regular saver investing in bank accounts is that inflation can quickly erode the value of your money.

7 Building Societies

Building societies offer one of the most popular ways of saving for small investors. Traditionally, they borrow money from the public to lend to people who want to buy their own homes. Should you be planning to buy a home sometime in the not too distant future, it may be a good idea to start saving with a society which is likely to lend you money on a property. This point is no longer as important as it used to be, but should still be one factor you consider when choosing your building society. Competition between banks and building societies is becoming more intense all the time and, since the building society cartel was abolished, the societies are free to fix their own investment rates and design new services. It is these two latter points which are of most interest to potential investors.

Many building society services compete directly with those of the banks and, as a result of new legislation, they are now able to offer cheque accounts and many are installing autobank machines. Some societies even offer overdraft facilities on their cheque accounts.

Your savings are very safe in a building society, particularly if it has been granted trustee status. This means that the society has met stringent requirements set out by the Chief Registrar of Building Societies. In the unlikely event that the society failed, the association would provide cover for investors, reimbursing 90 per cent of the amount invested in all accounts (apart from building society deposit accounts where 100 per cent reimbursement applies). For societies without trustee status, the Building Societies Association ('BSA') would reimburse 75 per cent of all monies deposited.

When choosing a building society a good tip is to check out the smaller, less popular societies in your area. You may well find their services are better suited to your needs and that the rates they offer savers are slightly higher than for the more popular societies because they don't spend so much on advertising. Other likely advantages include quicker and more personal service.

TAX TREATMENT

Building society interest is treated in the same way as bank interest for tax purposes. In other words, it is paid net of basic-rate tax, and higher-rate taxpayers are subject to tax at their marginal rate less basic-rate tax. Also, non-taxpayers cannot reclaim the tax paid. (Note, however, that this system is due to be radically altered from April 1991 – see the discussion of the new proposals at the start of Chapter Six.)

The only building society account which is treated differently is the second issue Save- As-You-Earn which is free of tax to the investor. We shall look at this scheme in closer detail later on in the chapter.

DEPOSIT ACCOUNTS

These accounts receive little if any publicity because they pay the lowest rate of interest available from building societies and it is easy to obtain a much higher return from other accounts.

The reason for the low interest rate is that deposit accounts are the safest of all building society accounts with holders entitled to the first claim against the assets of the society should it get into financial difficulty. But, as I have already mentioned, it is highly unlikely that this would happen to a BSA member and the vast majority of people are not prepared to take a much lower rate of interest for a marginally less risky investment. Let's now look at some of the more publicised accounts on offer from the building societies.

PAID-UP SHARE ACCOUNTS

These are probably the most popular and flexible of all the building society accounts. Sometimes called ordinary share accounts, they are very similar to bank deposit accounts. You can open an account with as little as £1 and add whatever you like whenever you like. You will normally receive a pass book in which all your transactions are recorded and interest is usually paid half-yearly. Withdrawals can be made on demand although a few days notice may be required for large amounts. Most societies limit cash withdrawals to around £250–£300.

These accounts can be extremely useful to very small savers and, over the years, it is possible to build up a reasonable sum of money. The interest rate paid is often slightly higher than the bank deposit account rate and building societies are open for longer hours than the banks (including Saturday opening which is not offered by all banks). Societies have tended to be much more accessible than banks making the paid-up share account, in particular, more flexible. If you shop around you may find higher interest rates from the smaller societies (anything up to one per cent more than the standard ordinary share account rate) but, on the other hand, they will probably not give you access to as wide a range of services.

Advantages

1. The same advantages as bank deposit accounts but with slightly higher interest.
2. Longer opening hours make these accounts more accessible.
3. Money is safe.
4. Ideal account for the very small investor who cannot always afford to save regular sums and needs the maximum flexibility.

Disadvantages

1. A higher return can be achieved elsewhere but at the expense of flexibility.

2. Interest received is rarely better than the rate of inflation.
3. Not suitable for non-taxpayers.
4. Once the account balance is £500 or more, you may well find a better return from another account.

CHILDREN'S ACCOUNTS

Like the banks, many building societies have accounts which aim to encourage children to save with them. Interest (net of tax) is earned on the money, often at paid-up share rates, and the societies also give away free gifts, although these tend to be slightly less impressive than from competing banks. The Woolwich, for instance, offers a pass book, a club magazine, a special pass book wallet and a card on the child's birthday. The age limit for these accounts is 12 and an account can be opened with just £1.

Advantages

1. As with the competing bank products, they encourage children to save.

Disadvantages

1. Not recommended as a vehicle for saving other than very small sums. Most children are non-taxpayers and better returns are available elsewhere.

SUBSCRIPTION SHARE ACCOUNTS

These are very flexible schemes for the regular saver with interest rates, depending on the society, anything up to 0.75 per cent above the paid-up share rate.

You must undertake to save regularly each month but you can vary the amounts to fit in with your other commitments. Some societies will let you save from as little as 10 pence per month, while the maximum is usually £250. There are no special restrictions on withdrawals and interest is usually added once a year. So as long as you deposit some money once a month, you will receive the more favourable return.

This really is an ideal account for the aspiring regular saver of any age, simply because it is so flexible. In practice, it allows you to save what you can, when you can, and still secure a more competitive rate of return. In addition, you can save for as long as you like and close the account whenever you like without any penalties. This kind of flexibility is not available with any of the regular savings products offered by the banks or, indeed, any other savings institutions. In fact, not all building societies offer subscription share accounts – but seek and you will find.

Because the minimum investment is extremely low, even children can be encouraged to use this account and benefit from a higher interest rate.

Advantages

1. Subscription share accounts are probably the most flexible accounts available anywhere for regular savers.
2. Some building societies set a minimum investment of as little as 10 pence per month.
3. There is no requirement laid down to invest a fixed amount each month and investors can vary their monthly subscription at will.
4. There is no fixed term.
5. A better rate of return is provided than on ordinary share accounts.

Disadvantages

1. The maximum monthly subscription is restricted to £250.
2. Once the subscription share account balance has reached £500, a better rate of return may be available elsewhere.
3. Non-taxpayers may be able to get a better return elsewhere, but this will generally be at the expense of flexibility.

MONTHLY SAVING OR MONEY BUILDER SCHEMES

These accounts are subtly different from those discussed earlier in this chapter and their terms and conditions tend to mirror those offered by the banks. There is often little to choose between the two institutions as far as the interest received is concerned. The rate is usually one per cent above the paid-up share account rate, although some soc- ieties offer more. Again you have to undertake to save regularly each month but this time it is a fixed amount – occasionally as little as £1 but often at least £10 per month. The maximums also vary between societies – usually £250 but sometimes £500 per month. You can increase monthly contributions in increments of £1 or decrease them, subject to the minimum, by the same amount. One partial withdrawal per year can be made, normally on demand, and some accounts allow you to miss up to four monthly payments without penalty. If you don't alter your payments or withdraw any money before the end of the year, some societies pay a bonus rate of interest. As with subscription share accounts, there is no maximum term.

These accounts are designed for the more committed regular saver who is prepared to accept less flexibility than is provided with subscription share accounts in return for a better rate of interest.

Advantages

1. An ideal account for the more disciplined saver.
2. A good way of saving for holidays or other specific items.
3. A better rate of return than on both ordinary and subscription share accounts.
4. Some of the monthly savings products offered by the building societies are more flexible than those offered by the banks. However, convenience and accessibility are often the only real advantages of the building society accounts.

Disadvantages

1. Non-taxpayers may find a better return elsewhere.

2. Once the account balance has reached £500, investors may find a higher interest rate with more flexibility elsewhere.

INSTANT ACCESS ACCOUNTS

Instant access accounts provide an excellent home for your emergency fund once it has reached a certain level. The minimum amount required to open an account is usually £1000, although some societies start at £500. You receive a premium rate of interest from 1.5–2 per cent above the ordinary share account rate and this increases as your balance reaches a higher band. Bands vary enormously between societies and it is very much a question of shopping around for the best return. The main feature of these accounts is that cash can be withdrawn instantly with no loss of interest – you do not have to give notice to get at your money.

If you have been saving regularly using a monthly savings account and your savings have reached a level at which you could open an instant access account, you may well be able to secure a better rate of interest while continuing to save as before. But should your account balance fall below the first band level, the interest paid will revert back to the ordinary share account rate. Once your balance entitles you to the second interest rate band, many societies offer the option to have interest paid monthly, so you can either spend it or leave it invested to earn interest on the interest. Without this monthly option, interest is often only paid annually or half-yearly. Exhibit 7.1 shows an example of a building society instant access account rate card.

Advantages

1. An excellent home for an emergency fund.
2. Savers using subscription share or monthly savings accounts should progress to this account once they reach the qualifying minimum because higher interest is usually available.

Exhibit 7.1 Building society instant access account rate card

Account	Investment	Net %	CAR[1]	Gross CAR[2]
Annual interest	£25000+	11.00	11.00	14.67
	£5000–£24999	10.75	10.75	14.33
	£1000–£4999	9.75	9.75	13.00
	Under £1000	6.75	6.75	9.00
Monthly interest	£25000+	10.48	11.00	14.67
	£5000–£24999	10.25	10.75	14.33

[1]Compounded annual rate when interest is added to the account.
[2]Gross equivalent to taxpayers at a basic rate of 25 per cent.
Source: Cheltenham & Gloucester Building Society (1st March, 1990).

3. Instant access to your money without loss of interest.
4. Very competitive interest rates paid.

Disadvantages

1. Non-taxpayers can obtain better returns elsewhere but often at the expense of flexibility.
2. If your balance falls below the first band level, interest will revert to the ordinary share account rate.
3. Only in recent years have these accounts given a return higher than inflation. Over the long term this has not been the case.

NOTICE ACCOUNTS

Not so long ago, lots of the societies had a range of notice accounts (for example, requiring 7 or 28 days notice of withdrawals). Many of these have now been discontinued in favour of a single 90 day account with withdrawals subject to 90 days notice or loss of 90 days interest on amounts withdrawn without notice. This feature is the only major difference between notice and instant access accounts. In return for the more limited flexibility, a higher interest rate is paid based on the same interest bands. However, some societies do allow instant withdrawals without loss of interest provided the remaining balance is in excess of a certain figure, usually £10,000. Also, a monthly interest option is available on the second interest band upwards.

These accounts are mainly of benefit to substantial savers. Those with a sum in excess of £10,000 are able to obtain a higher rate of interest while still having instant access to their funds above the £10,000 band without penalty.

Advantages

1. These accounts offer close to the best return available for your cash.
2. Many societies now allow you instant access to your money provided a minimum balance of £10,000 is maintained in your account.
3. A monthly income option is often available.

Disadvantages

1. Not suitable for the small saver because of the 90 days notice or loss of interest on withdrawals.
2. Tax paid cannot be reclaimed by the investor.

CHEQUE BOOK ACCOUNTS

The building societies are now starting to provide interest-bearing cheque accounts which are operated in the same way as bank current accounts with the advantage that your money earns interest. We have already discussed under bank accounts (Chapter Six) how useful a cheque account can be to most of us, and how its features can be very helpful to the regular saver.

You can open one of these current accounts with just £1 and the interest is calculated daily and credited to your account at the beginning of each month. Although the rates paid vary, they are usually a fraction less than the ordinary share account rate. There are no transaction charges and overdraft facilities (subject, of course, to interest charges) are available by arrangement. Otherwise these accounts have similar features to bank current accounts in that you will receive regular statements, a cheque guarantee card and, in many cases, a cash card service as well.

A note of caution when shopping around for a building society interest-bearing cheque account concerns the fact that some societies offer a cheque book facility, but only in conjunction with one of their savings accounts. When the balance on the cheque book account falls below a specified amount it is topped up from the savings account and, if it goes above a certain level, money is automatically transferred into the savings account. Interest will only be paid on the money in the savings account and, to my mind, these are not interest-bearing cheque accounts in the strict sense.

Advantages

1. As with bank current accounts but with the added advantage of interest.
2. You receive interest on money set aside for paying bills by direct debit and standing order before these sums are paid.

Disadvantages

1. Not recommended as a vehicle for saving in itself because better returns are available elsewhere.

SECOND ISSUE SAVE-AS-YOU-EARN

This is normally abbreviated to '2nd issue SAYE' and provides a way of turning as little as 70 pence per week into hundreds of pounds. It is a monthly savings plan, only available from building societies, which is controlled by the UK Treasury. Unlike all other building society accounts, the return on the scheme is free of income tax and capital gains tax to the investor.

Anyone over 16 can take out a contract with the building society and will be required to make 60 payments (i.e. 1 a month for 5 years). At the end of the 5-year period a bonus is added equal to 14 extra payments and if you leave the money in the scheme for an additional 2 years without further payments, the bonus is doubled to 28 monthly payments. The minimum investment is £1 per month and the maximum is £20.

The returns on this investment can be very attractive as is illustrated in Exhibit 7.2. The 5-year bonus is equivalent to an effective annual rate of interest of 8.62 per cent. In order to accumulate the same return after the deduction of tax, a basic-rate taxpayer would have to find a gross return of 11.07 per cent for the 5-year bonus and 11.49 per cent for the 7-year bonus. The top-rate taxpayer would need to achieve a gross return of 13.83 per cent for the 5-year bonus and 14.37 per cent for the 7-year bonus. This clearly makes the scheme very attractive indeed for higher-rate taxpayers who should make as much use of it as possible.

The rules governing the contract are strict but do not make the scheme totally inflexible. For instance, if during the five-year period an instalment is missed, the contract is extended by one month. Up to six instalments can be

Exhibit 7.2 Returns on the 2nd issue SAYE scheme (in £s)

Amount saved per month	*Amount saved after 5 years*	*Savings + 5-year bonus*	*Savings + 7-year bonus*
1	60	74	88
3	180	222	264
5	300	370	440
10	600	740	880
15	900	1110	1320
20	1200	1480	1760

missed with a resultant extension of the contract by six months. If more than six instalments are missed then the amount returned depends on how long the contract has been in existence. If the contract is broken during the first year only the amount paid in is repaid. If it is broken between years one and five then the amount paid in, plus tax-free interest at six per cent per annum is repaid.

The 2nd issue SAYE scheme is an excellent investment for the very small regular saver because many of the banks and building societies are beginning to insist on a minimum investment of £10 per month for their monthly savings plans. In addition, the interest paid on other regular savings plans is rarely anything like as good as on the SAYE scheme. There is a very low monthly minimum – £3 per month, for example, works out at just 70 pence per week over a full year. Exhibit 7.2 shows that after the 5-year bonus has been added you have turned just 70 pence per week into £222. We can all turn pennies into worthwhile sums of money if we are prepared to plan and stick with it.

The SAYE scheme is also extremely attractive to higher-rate taxpayers. Most would find it easy to contribute the maximum £20 per month in order to secure about the best guaranteed return available. Alternatively, higher-rate taxpayers can decide to deposit £1200 with the building society which takes the instalments out of this sum and pays the investor interest on the decreasing balance. I believe the SAYE scheme is an excellent way of saving money and deserves to be far more popular than it is – and it is a must for all higher-rate taxpayers.

Advantages

1. A guaranteed return on your money.
2. Gives an excellent return to higher-rate taxpayers.
3. Even extremely small savers can afford to enter this scheme and benefit from the attractive returns.
4. An extremely safe investment.
5. When inflation is low you achieve a real return on your investment.

Disadvantages

1. You have to be older than 16 years to start a contract.
2. Restricted to a maximum of £20 per month.
3. Not very flexible and therefore best suited as a medium- to long-term investment.
4. A contract must run for more than one year to secure a return on your money.

SUMMARY

Many of the services offered by the building societies compete directly with those of the banks and therefore the pros and cons tend to be similar. The societies provide an excellent home for your emergency fund as well as short- to medium-term savings. Apart from the 2nd issue SAYE, their products are taxed in the same way as those of the banks. It is only a personal view but I find that the societies tend to give a more friendly and individual service and are more accessible than the banks. As competition between the two institutions inevitably becomes more fierce, there is likely to be less and less to choose between them, so it is very much a question of personal preferences and shopping around for what you want.

8 National Savings

This is the government sector of the savings market offering a range of excellent products for the saver and investor. Many higher-rate taxpayers are well aware of the substantial benefits provided by some of these products but smaller savers do not always appreciate their usefulness and importance.

In part, this could be because of the unexciting image conjured up in many people's minds by National Savings. This may have been justifiable in the past when the prime concern was investment safety: it is highly unlikely that the government would default on its obligations and it used to be that investors paid for the extra security through lower interest rates. All that has changed because banks and building societies now offer comparable security and National Savings has to compete with them for savers' money by offering attractive returns. Until recently, National Savings also enjoyed an advantage from the fact that their products are sold at post offices – open for longer weekday hours than the banks, and on Saturday mornings. Both the banks and the building societies are now extending their opening hours to counteract this.

National Savings probably has at least one product in its range to suit everyone, but I will discuss only those that might be considered by the regular saver and investor.

ORDINARY ACCOUNT

The procedure to open one of these accounts is simply to go to your post office and fill in an application form. The minimum deposit at any time is £5 and the maximum account balance is normally £10,000. Once the account is open, holders receive a bank book in which all transactions and the account balance are recorded. Withdrawals can be made of up to £100 per day on demand. Interest up to £70 is tax free and so for most savers there is no bother about tax. Above all your investment is completely safe.

The interest rate structure is quite complicated and operates on two levels. The structure is announced towards the end of each year and rates are guaranteed for the whole of the following year, regardless of movements in other rates. The guaranteed rates for 1990 are 2.5 per cent gross on balances below £500 and 5 per cent gross on balances of £500 or more, provided this balance is retained throughout the calender year (i.e from 31st December, 1989 to 1st January, 1991). If your balance drops below £500 you will only receive the lower rate. Interest is earned on whole pounds on deposit for complete calendar months. Money does not earn interest in the month of deposit, nor in the month in which it is withdrawn, so the best thing is to make deposits at the end of a month and withdrawals at the beginning of a month. Interest is automatically credited to accounts on 31st December each year.

As mentioned, you can withdraw up to £100 on demand, but if you withdraw more than £50 in cash the bank book is kept for checking. Larger amounts can be obtained within a few days on application to the National Savings Bank in Glasgow. Once you have used your account for six months, you can exceed the normal cash limit by applying for a regular customer account at your chosen post office. You can then draw £250 in cash without having to hand in your bank book.

This account, therefore, has a lot of complications and it is not easy to get the best use out of it. Interest rates are very low indeed on balances below £500, and even £70 tax-free interest to a 40 per cent taxpayer is not particularly attractive (a gross rate of only 8.33 per cent before deduction of tax). So ordinary accounts have very limited appeal to regular savers who will also need to ensure that deposits and withdrawals are carefully timed to obtain the maximum interest on their money.

Advantages

1. Guaranteed interest rates no matter what happens to other rates. Advantageous when rates in general are coming down.
2. Minimum deposit only £5.
3. First £70 of interest tax free. Interest in excess of £70 is paid without deduction of basic-rate tax.
4. Very accessible through the post office.
5. Completely safe investment.
6. Instant access to cash up to £100 or, if conditions are met, up to £250.
7. Accounts can be opened in the names of children under the age of seven but withdrawals are not permitted until the child reaches seven.

Disadvantages

1. Cumbersome in operation.
2. Timing of investment and withdrawals critical.
3. Very low rate of return on your money. Despite interest being paid gross, a non-taxpayer would probably obtain a better return from a building society instant-access account.
4. Much better returns available elsewhere.
5. You cannot deposit less than £5.

INVESTMENT ACCOUNT

This account is also available from the post office, but it offers a far more attractive return. At the time of writing it is 12.75 per cent per annum (increased from 11.75 per cent on 3rd April, 1990) and, unlike bank and building society interest, it is paid gross. This return is equivalent to 9.56 per cent net of basic-rate tax at 25 per cent. Investment account interest is taxable but tax is not deducted at source – a big advantage for people who are not liable to tax. The minimum deposit at any time is £5 and the maximum account balance is £25,000, although this figure may be exceeded by interest credited. Interest is automatically credited to your account on 31st

December each year. It is calculated on a daily basis and earned on each whole pound for each day it is held on deposit. An important condition of investment accounts is that investors must give one month's notice of withdrawal. Withdrawals cannot be made on demand under any circumstances, so it is advisable to have some money easily available in another account in order to cover immediate needs.

This account is excellent for non-taxpayers – arguably the best. It is also very attractive for regular savers, even if they are basic-rate taxpayers. You can save a minimum of £5 regularly, and using the 'Save by Post' facility you do not have to go to the post office every time.

It is only when the balance reaches £1000 that the basic-rate taxpayer will find comparable returns elsewhere, and the balance will probably need to be around £5000 before the return can be bettered. The only constraint on regular savers is the need to give one month's notice of withdrawals and the minimum deposit requirement of £5. Comparison with bank and building society monthly savings accounts, however, shows the investment account to be a relatively flexible product offering very good returns for both basic-rate and non-taxpayers.

Advantages

1. Your savings are absolutely secure.
2. The best savings account for non-taxpayers.
3. Basic-rate taxpayers who save small sums on a regular basis will find the returns very hard to beat.
4. Very accessible across the post office counter and through the mail.
5. An excellent account for children.

Disadvantages

1. Withdrawals require one month's notice.
2. You will need to keep some money aside in another instant-access account to cover immediate needs.
3. You cannot deposit less than £5.

PREMIUM BONDS

The electronic random number indicator equipment ('ERNIE') regularly picks premium bond numbers and pays out tax-free prizes to bond holders. It can be argued that everyone should invest at least the minimum amount in premium bonds so that they have a chance, no matter how remote, of winning the big prize. I think it is important to at least consider premium bonds as a method of putting money aside regularly, even if it is unsuitable for most people.

Premium bonds enable savers to enter a regular draw for tax-free prizes whilst retaining the right to get their money back. This right separates premium bond investment from gambling, or all-out speculation, where your original stake money is at risk. Your money is paid into a fund and a sum equivalent to interest on the fund is put into a prize fund and distributed by weekly and monthly prize draws. The prizes are free of all UK income and capital gains tax.

Bonds are in units of £1 and the minimum purchase for bond holders aged 16 or over is £100 (£10 for under-16s). Above these amounts, you can buy bonds in multiples of £10 up to a maximum holding of £10,000 per person. Bonds become eligible for prizes once they have been held for three clear calendar months following the month of purchase. Therefore, a bond bought at the end of January would first become eligible for the draws in May. Each £1 unit has a separate chance in the draw and the prizes make impressive reading. Every week there are single jackpot prizes of £100,000, £50,000 and £25,000 and, every month, more than 200,000 prizes in the £50 to £5000 range plus a big monthly jackpot prize of £250,000. Every prize winner is notified by post at the last address recorded at the Bonds and Stock Office and over the years thousands of prizes have gone unclaimed because people have failed to inform ERNIE of their change of address.

So what are the chances of winning a prize? A recent advertisement says that, given statistically average luck, someone holding £1000 worth of bonds may expect to win a prize every year and a holding of £10,000 should win 10 prizes a year. Apparently the odds of someone with the maximum £10,000 holding not winning a prize in any one year are a staggering 55,000 to 1. If a person holding the maximum has average luck and wins 10 of the minimum £50 prizes a year, their net return is 5 per cent per annum. A 40 per cent taxpayer would have to secure a return, before tax, of 8.33 per cent in order to achieve the same result.

So premium bonds could turn out to be a disastrous investment or an extremely good one, but two things are certain – you can always get your original investment back and, as time passes, inflation will erode its value.

The minimum purchase level of £100 puts premium bonds, as a regular investment, beyond the reach of many people over the age of 16 (although the minimum of £10 for under-16s is attractive). A premium bond holding gives you a chance to win a really big prize – but it is just a chance and does not mean that you will win. Savers need to consider if they can afford to accept not winning a prize and going without interest on their money. Not only that, but over time, inflation will erode the value of the original investment. If you can afford to accept these conditions, and not all of us can, then do go ahead. If you are lucky enough to win a prize why not re-invest it into premium bonds and increase your chances of further wins – just treat the prize as money you never had unless, of course, you win a big prize. Whatever you decide, I wish you good luck.

Advantages

1. Your original stake is completely safe and repayable in full.
2. Any winnings are free of all UK income and capital gains tax.
3. The bonds are readily available and only eight working days notice is required for withdrawals.
4. It may turn out to be the best investment you ever made.

Disadvantages

1. Your original investment will be eroded by inflation.
2. There is no guarantee that you will ever win a prize.
3. Only suitable for those who can afford to lose interest on their money in the hope of winning a good prize.
4. You must keep the bond for three clear calendar months before it is eligible to take part in a prize draw.
5. Not recommended as a way of building up capital. It is much better to use a plan that gives a good return on your money.
6. The minimum initial purchase of £100 reduces the appeal of premium bonds as a regular investment.
7. It may turn out to be one of the worst investments you have made.

YEARLY PLAN

The yearly plan is a National Savings regular investment scheme offering guaranteed and tax-free returns. These returns are usually very competitive and, because they are completely tax free, this scheme is extremely attractive for all taxpayers, particularly those paying higher-rate tax.

The investor agrees to make monthly payments for one year. At the end of that year a yearly plan certificate is issued to the value of the payments plus the interest they have earned. This certificate then earns a higher rate of interest. The maximum guaranteed rate of interest is earned if the certificate is held for a further four full years. The guaranteed tax free return over the full five years is currently 7.5 per cent per annum (see Exhibit 8.1).

There is an interest rate band between the date of issue of the certificate to two years and four years. These rates are shown on the offer letter sent to you when you apply for the yearly plan.

The minimum monthly payment is £20 increasing by £5 steps to a maximum of £200. The payments have to be made by standing order and the investor will receive confirmation of the guaranteed rates that will be paid on receipt of the application form. These rates are guaranteed

Exhibit 8.1 Yearly plan percentage returns

Period	*Return (%)*
Year 1	5.75
Year 2	7.75
Year 3	7.75
Year 4	7.75
Year 5	7.75
Full 5 years	7.50

Note: The 'Year 1' percentage represents the annual interest on each monthly payment in the first year. Years 2–5 show what the certificate will earn *if it is kept for another 4 years.*

Exhibit 8.2 Yearly plan guaranteed cash returns

Investment in first year (if twelve payments are made)	*Certificate value when issued (at end of first year)*	*Tax-free value of certificate after five years*
£240 (12x£20)	£247.48	£333.59
£300 (12x£25)	£309.35	£416.98
£360 (12x£30)	£371.22	£500.38
£420 (12x£35)	£433.09	£583.78
£480 (12x£40)	£494.95	£667.16
£540 (12x£45)	£556.82	£750.56
£600 (12x£50)	£618.69	£833.95
£660 (12x£55)	£680.56	£917.35
£720 (12x£60)	£742.43	£1000.75
£840 (12x£70)	£866.17	£1167.54
£960 (12x£80)	£989.90	£1334.32
£1200 (12x£100)	£1237.38	£1667.91
£2400 (12x£200)	£2474.75	£3335.80

Note: This information is correct at the time of going to press.
Source: Crown copyright. Reproduced by permission of the Director of Savings.

for the full duration of the plan no matter what happens to interest rates generally. Each year you have the option to carry on saving to buy a further certificate, to stop the plan, or to apply to start a new plan with a different contribution. The returns are less attractive if you cash in your plan early. No interest is earned on monthly payments repaid before the end of the first year.

Although the yearly plan is for regular savers, there is no long-term commitment to save because the agreement is renewable annually. This in itself makes it very flexible when you are looking for a medium- to long-term savings plan. Also, you know exactly what your return will be from the outset. You can even use the yearly plan for a saving or income scheme which is self-financing after year five, as illustrated in Exhibit 8.3.

As shown in the exhibit, the scheme works like this: you make regular payments for five years and when the first plan matures you can use the proceeds to make regular payments to fund a new plan in year six. You would have a choice of re-investing just your original investment and taking the tax-free profit as income, or re-investing the total return on your money, subject to the maximum investment limit. As the proceeds are invested by monthly instalments, you would pay the lump sum into an interest-bearing account, thereby making even more use of your money.

Advantages

1. All returns are tax free.
2. Rates of return are guaranteed over five years.
3. Your savings are completely safe.
4. Although ideally suited to regular savers, there is no long-term commitment to save for more than one year.
5. Attractive rates of return for all investors but more especially for higher-rate taxpayers. All higher-rate taxpayers should take out this plan.
6. Anyone over seven years old can apply to take out a plan.

Exhibit 8.3 Using the yearly plan to accumulate capital or produce tax-free income

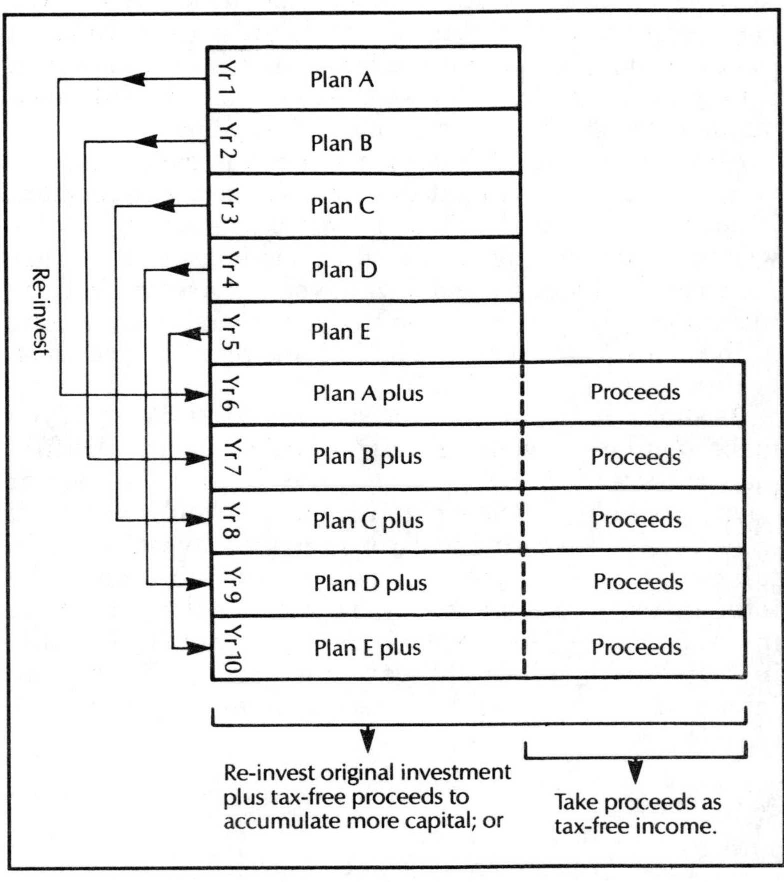

Disadvantages

1. Best return only available over the full five years.
2. No interest is earned on monthly payments repaid in the first year.
3. Better returns are possible elsewhere but rates are not guaranteed.
4. Over the long term, returns are unlikely to beat inflation.

SAVINGS CERTIFICATES

Although the yearly plan offers a way of buying a saving certificate on a monthly basis, there are two more readily recognisable forms of saving certificates: those offering a fixed, guaranteed initial return; and index-linked certificates, which earn interest over and above inflation-proofing.

34th ISSUE SAVINGS CERTIFICATES – A GUARANTEED FIXED RETURN

This is the issue of certificates available at the time of writing and they guarantee a compound annual interest rate of 7.5 per cent over their full 5-year term. They are purchased in whole units, each costing £25, and you may hold up to 40 units or £1000 worth. This is in addition to all holdings of other issues of savings certificates you may own. There are also special facilities for holding up to £10,000 in 34th issue certificates if you are re-investing from earlier issues of certificates, including index-linked issues. Earlier issues must have been held for at least five years.

The return on these certificates is guaranteed and completely tax free. However, if repayment is made during the first year then normally only the purchase price is repaid (although an exception covers re-investment from earlier issues of certificates). Exhibit 8.4 shows the return you can expect if certificates, held for at least one year, are cashed, up to and including the fifth anniversary of purchase.

If you keep your certificates for more than 5 years they will start to earn interest at what is called the 'general extension rate', currently 5.01 per cent per annum tax free. In order to make it attractive to re-invest old certificates into 're-investment certificates', you will receive a return of six per cent for each three-month period if you cash these certificates within one year. After that, the early encashment rates are the same as set out in Exhibit 8.4.

Fixed return saving certificates offer a very competitive rate, and because the interest paid is tax free they are

Exhibit 8.4 34th issue – certificate encashment rates

Date of repayment	*Compound interest*[1]
On or after 1st anniversary of purchase but before 2nd	6.00% p.a.
On or after 2nd anniversary of purchase but before 3rd	6.25% p.a.
On or after 3rd anniversary of purchase but before 4th	6.50% p.a.
On or after 4th anniversary of purchase but before 5th	7.00% p.a.
At 5th anniversary of purchase date	7.50% p.a.

[1]The compound interest earned from the date of purchase.
Note: This information is correct at the time of going to press.
Source: Crown copyright. Reproduced by permission of the Director of Savings.

particularly attractive to the higher-rate taxpayer. As far as the regular saver is concerned, it is possible to invest £25 at a time. The advantage of saving like this is that the saver knows exactly what each unit will be worth after 5 years (in this case £35.89 – see Exhibit 8.5).

Advantages

1. You receive a guaranteed tax-free rate of return.
2. Competitive rates make the certificates extremely attractive for the higher-rate taxpayer.
3. Guaranteed return makes this investment especially attractive in times of decreasing interest rates.
4. No age limits on holders.

Disadvantages

1. The return is not guaranteed to beat inflation.
2. No return on investment if cashed within one year.
3. Not ideally suited to all regular savers because of the £25 unit minimum, although you can save when you like.

Exhibit 8.5 34th issue returns after 5 years

Purchase price	*Value after 5 years*	*Total return over 5 years*
£25	£35.89	£10.89
£100	£143.56	£43.56
£500	£717.81	£217.81
£1000	£1435.63	£435.63

FOURTH ISSUE INDEX-LINKED CERTIFICATES

Index-linked certificates match changes in prices (i.e. they are inflation-proofed) and pay guaranteed extra interest on an increasing scale each year for up to five years. This means that not only is your capital protected against inflation but you receive an additional overall return over the five years of 4.04 per cent a year tax free (see Exhibit 8.6).

As with other saving certificates, only the sum invested is repaid if you cash in before the first anniversary. That aside, inflation-proofing and extra interest are earned monthly from the date of purchase. The index-linked return and the guaranteed extra interest (both completely tax free) are capitalised annually, so that in the second

Exhibit 8.6 Fourth index-linked issue certificates – returns over and above inflation

Period	*Return*
Year 1	3.00%
Year 2	3.25%
Year 3	3.50%
Year 4	4.50%
Year 5	6.00%

Note: Equivalent to an overall 5-year return of 4.04% per annum on top of inflation proofing.

year this new total earns index linking and additional interest, itself capitalised at the end of the second year, and so on. The index-linking rate is tied to changes in the annual Retail Prices Index or RPI, announced monthly. The RPI applicable to a particular month is the figure issued by the government in the previous month (so, for example, the RPI applicable to a purchase of certificates in April would be the figure announced in March). Again you must purchase the certificates in whole units of £25. The minimum holding is one unit (£25) and the maximum is 200 units (£5000).

It is extremely rare to come across an investment that guarantees the value of your savings against the ravages of inflation. Appreciating how difficult it is to get a 'real' return on your money with ordinary interest-bearing investments is very important. The inflation table in Chapter Two (Exhibit 2.2) showed how quickly even a low inflation rate can erode the value of savings. Inflation hurts small savers most and having made provision for emergency money and long-term objectives, the first home everyone should consider for their medium-term money is index-linked savings certificates. Even in times of low inflation, index linking makes this investment one of the best around for all savers but, again, the tax-free status makes it most attractive to higher-rate taxpayers.

Advantages

1. One of the few investments to guarantee a return to match the rate of inflation.
2. Extra interest on top of index linking at a guaranteed rate.
3. This investment is a must in times of high inflation.
4. Repayments are free of all UK income and capital gains tax.
5. After five years the certificates will earn interest at a variable rate, as well as inflation-proofing, until further notice.
6. No age limits on holders.

Disadvantages

1. Only the sum invested is returned if certificates are cashed within the first year.

SUMMARY

In this chapter I have only examined National Savings products that the regular saver might consider. Some of the products pay interest without deducting tax, which makes them extremely attractive to non-taxpayers (e.g. most children). The investment account offers excellent value and is even attractive to many basic-rate taxpayers.

Other returns are totally tax free and higher-rate taxpayers should make maximum use of these products. Index-linked certificates are so important that I believe most people should place at least a portion of their savings into this excellent product.

Whenever you have any extra funds to invest it is always worth visiting the post office and keeping up to date with the schemes provided by National Savings before considering the bank or building society alternatives. The only criticism of National Savings products is that if you do not keep strictly within the rules then the penalties can be harsh. Also, some of the schemes still suffer from being rather awkward and cumbersome to operate as far as regular savers are concerned.

9 Insurance Products

The word insurance conjures up so many negative images in most people's minds that my guess is you have seen the title of this chapter, flicked through to see how long it is, and have promptly switched off. I am convinced that 'insurance' is one of the few remaining taboo subjects in the English language. But, believe it or not, you will suffer no serious illness as a result of reading this chapter – in fact, you should be able to pick up some useful knowledge on how to profit from investing in insurance products.

So far in this book we have only considered short- to medium-term savings in cash investments. The regular savings products available from the insurance industry are invariably long-term investments, carrying rather more risk than the savings vehicles discussed earlier. Investment has a higher risk and longer time-scale than saving, with returns coming in the form of income, capital gains, or a mixture of the two. It follows therefore, that you can only start to tackle your long-term investment goals after you have made adequate provision to meet unforeseen financial emergencies, such as redundancy or a large repair bill for the car.

There are many insurance products which make excellent homes for your long-term investments and savings, and which are ideally suited to achieving your long-term goals. But for most people insurance conjures up the idea of paying an exorbitant amount of money to an insurance company to cover you for an event which almost certainly will never happen – and if it does happen you have difficulty in getting your money. This is why many people compare insurance to putting money down the drain. Others appreciate the security which insurance provides but, nonetheless, view it as no more than a necessary evil – just another bill that has to be paid.

Not only do many people treat all insurance policies with suspicion, but they tend to view the people who sell them with equal misgivings, mainly because the sales people receive commission on every policy they sell. For some reason insurance sales people have acquired a dreadful reputation, provoking hostile reactions from a sizeable proportion of the population. The image of the friendly man from the 'Pru', with his rusty bicycle clips, may have disappeared along with his bicycle, but the same friendly sales people are still around.

We have touched on just a few of the negative ways in which people react to insurance generally, but why should they react in the same way to life assurance when it can be such a good investment? It's worth thinking about taboo subjects for a moment. All of us at some time have found ourselves lost for words when we have met a close friend whose mother or father has just died. Similarly, we find it difficult to ask our friends how much money they earn and, even if we did, I imagine most would still keep us guessing. The truth is, the average person finds it difficult to talk about death or money – what hope is there of getting them to discuss both subjects at once under the heading 'life insurance'? If you react to life insurance with a shudder it may be worth going back for a quick refresher to the 'Change of attitude' section in Chapter One. If we look at life insurance in a positive way it soon becomes apparent that it can be an extremely flexible and profitable weapon in the regular saver's arsenal.

LIFE INSURANCE BASICS

Life insurance has two main uses – protection and savings. Some policies are designed for protection only and vice versa, but you can, of course, combine the two qualities of saving and protection in the same policy. Protection-type policies provide the beneficiaries of the life assured with a guaranteed sum of money should the life assured die within a set period, but nothing if they survive the period. If a policy pays out at a set date or, alternatively, at earlier death, then it is a savings vehicle as well. So you know exactly what money your beneficiaries will receive if you die within a set time period, and you also know what money you will receive if you survive the period.

We are all going to die – it is just a question of when – so here, unlike other forms of insurance, we are not insuring against an unlikely event. Also, disputed claims are unlikely: it is difficult even for an insurance company to prove a dead person to be alive. It is true that when you die you will never see your money back, but your beneficiaries will, and they can use it to help them through a difficult time.

WHAT IS A POLICY?

There are three parties to a life insurance policy: the proposer; the life assured; and the beneficiary. The proposer is the person who pays the premium to the insurance company. The life assured is the person on whose life the policy is based. If the life assured dies, then the proposer does not pay any more premiums and the insurance company will pay out the sum due to the named beneficiary. In many cases, the proposer and the life assured will be the same individual – for instance, with a protection-type policy, a husband, while his wife would be the beneficiary. If, however, the policy is the type that pays out at a set date it would be acceptable for the husband to be the beneficiary as well. In this case the policy would also be a savings vehicle.

THE PREMIUM

Let us first of all examine what makes a premium cheap or expensive. The insurance company has to take into account the risk of the life assured dying, and the factors that affect this are health and age. Generally, the younger you are when you take out life insurance, the cheaper the premiums. Your sex also affects the cost of premiums because women tend to live longer than men. Insurance

Exhibit 9.1 Initial period of a policy for commission purposes

Term of premium	*Initial period*
10 years	16 months
15 years	24 months
20 years	31 months
25 years	38 months

companies usually treat women as younger than men at the same age and therefore their premiums are cheaper. On a conventional policy the level of premium is set relative to the age of the life assured at the outset of the policy. The older the applicant is when taking out the policy then the more expensive the premiums become.

As well as the cost of protection, the premiums also have to cover the insurance company's administrative expenses, such as office back-up, staff and advertising costs. Also, many life insurance sales people are paid on a commission basis. Commissions are usually split into two categories: initial and renewal.

The initial commission paid depends on how long the initial period of a policy runs, and the longer the term of the policy the longer the initial period (see Exhibit 9.1). Commission of 25 per cent of each premium in the initial period is payable. For example, on a 15-year endowment assurance, initial commission is calculated on the first 24 months. Therefore, if the premium is £20 per month, initial commission of £120 is payable (i.e. £5 x 24). These are guidelines set out by the regulatory organisation and, although many companies base their commission structure on these guidelines, some may pay all the initial commission in the first year, or may even pay a higher rate. In the above example, the rate would work out at 50 per cent of the first year's premium. After the initial period, renewal commission is payable at a rate of 2.5 per cent for the remaining years that the premium is payable. The reason why so much commission accrues early on is that surprisingly few policies reach their maturity dates – they are cashed in long before.

If you have a savings-type policy, yet another portion of your premium will have to be set aside for the investment content of the policy. In the first two years your policy would typically have little or no value because, as we have seen, the insurance company has to cover the risk of you dying and it also costs a lot to set up a policy. It is only when the risk and most expenses have been covered that more and more of your premium goes towards the investment part of the policy. This highlights the point I made earlier – these life assurance savings plans are invariably long-term investments and in the early years your policy will have a very low surrender (or cash in) value. In the first five years it would be unusual to get back more than you have paid in. These policies only really start to perform after about eight years and you will only get the maximum benefit if you hold them to maturity – i.e. for the full term of the policy.

Exhibit 9.2 illustrates the surrender value of a policy during each of the first five years. This particular policy has an initial premium of £30 per month which increases at the end of each year by 7 per cent of the initial regular monthly amount. The values set out in the table have been calculated according to rules prescribed by LAUTRO (the

Exhibit 9.2 An illustration of policy surrender values

		Surrender values (£s) for male aged at entry		
Years in force	*Premiums paid (£s)*	*34 years*	*54 years*	*74 years*
1	331.00	198	173	68
2	716.20	551	491	254
3	1126.60	937	841	465
4	1562.20	1415	1283	771
5	2023.00	1948	1784	1148

Life Assurance and Unit Trust Regulatory Organisation), and are not necessarily the actual values you would receive because this depends on the bonuses added to the policy (discussed later) and the surrender basis current at the time. What it does demonstrate, however, is that if you cash in your policy within five years you will probably get back less than you have put in. In addition, the older you are when you start the policy the lower the cash-in value for the same number of years as a younger person. This is because more money is required to pay for death benefits as the age of the life assured increases at entry.

It is very important, therefore, not to overload yourself with assurance and to make sure you can easily afford the premiums – if you have to give up a policy before it has run its course, the penalties are very heavy indeed.

Having looked at how premiums are apportioned by the insurance companies (protection, expenses and investment), I should now explain the main types of policy, moving on to discuss how we can make the best and most profitable use of them.

Life insurance policies fall into three main categories. Two of these (term and whole life policies) are protection-type policies and only the beneficiaries, not the life assured, receive any money. The third type (endowment policies) provides for either the beneficiaries or the life assured, if the latter survives to the maturity date of the policy. This category offers both a protection and an investment element and can be particularly useful to regular savers.

TERM INSURANCE

This is the cheapest form of life cover available. The policy only pays out if the life assured dies before a set date and, if they survive beyond this date, then nothing is paid out. Premiums are usually paid monthly for the period or 'term' of the policy, commonly 10 years. If the life assured dies within that period the beneficiary will receive a pre-set, guaranteed sum. As a guide, a premium of £2.50 per month over 10 years should cover a man aged 30 next birthday for £10,000. A man aged 40 next birthday taking out a similar policy would expect to pay around £4.10 per month over 10 years. Your maximum age at the start of these policies is generally set at either 60 or 65, depending on the particular insurance company. Many of the modern term assurance policies are renewable, meaning that they provide the opportunity to renew the plan without having to give the insurance company any evidence of your state of health.

Term insurance is purely a protection-type policy and can be found marketed under different names, the most common being mortgage protection and family protection policies. Banks and building societies often insist that borrowers with repayment mortgages take out a mortgage protection policy so that the proceeds from the policy will pay off the mortgage if the borrower dies before the end of the mortgage term.

Family protection policies provide the surviving spouse with enough capital or income to maintain their standard of living. The major insurance companies all have plans under which the policy would provide your family with a regular tax-free income every three months from the date of your death until the end of the chosen term. For example, if you choose a 20-year term and an income benefit of £10,000 per annum, if death occurs 10 years after starting the policy then your family would receive a tax-free income of £10,000 per annum for the remaining 10 years of the policy.

Be careful when choosing the level of benefits with family protection policies. An income of £10,000 per year may seem reasonable now, but 10 or 15 years of inflation can severely reduce its value. It is important to review your policies at least every five years and preferably more often. You may need to top them up. Alternatively, look for a company which offers the facility of an increasing income benefit under which the amount payable increases by a set percentage per annum. This will help offset the effects of inflation.

WHOLE LIFE INSURANCE

This type of policy pays out a guaranteed sum on the death of the life assured. There is no pay out during the time the life assured is alive and therefore it is not a savings vehicle that he or she can benefit from. The cost of this form of life cover is more than for term cover because the insurance company will have to pay out at some time.

Whole life insurance is available in a variety of forms. First, there is the without-profits contract which provides the maximum immediate, permanent level of guaranteed death benefit for a minimal cost. As I mentioned earlier, the effects of inflation over a long period can render the death benefit on this type of policy inadequate and therefore I would advise that you should always choose a with-profits contract. With-profits contracts require the payment of a higher premium but the policy participates in the profits of the company so that the benefit payable on death increases year by year with the addition of any declared bonuses arising from these profits. Over a period of years these additions to the sum assured help to counteract the effects of inflation. With some whole life policies you don't have to pay your premiums for the whole of your life – some companies allow you to stop paying once you have reached your 65th year. This is a useful feature because after retirement it may become less easy to keep up the premium payments.

Whole life insurance is not as popular as it used to be because many modern plans offer more flexibility. Its major use, however, is to provide a cash sum to pay for inheritance tax, to which end the whole life policy is particularly well suited.

ENDOWMENT POLICIES

These policies can be split into two major categories: with- or without-profits. In both cases the policy pays out a guaranteed minimum sum on maturity or on the death of the life assured, whichever occurs first.

WITHOUT-PROFITS ENDOWMENT POLICIES

These are the cheaper of the two types of endowment policy as they *only* pay out a set sum on maturity or earlier death. As with other policies, you normally pay premiums monthly for a fixed number of years. The premiums are more expensive than for a whole life policy because the guaranteed sum has a known pay-out date, commonly 10 or 25 years from taking out the policy.

Without-profits endowment policies offer regular savers a poor return on their money. The only advantage to this investment is that you are guaranteed a sum of money at a set time in the future and so, for example, it is a very safe and convenient way of paying off a mortgage. A far better return can be obtained from with-profits policies which offer many very good ways for the regular saver to build up a useful sum.

WITH-PROFITS ENDOWMENT POLICIES

These policies offer an excellent method for the regular saver to build up a substantial capital sum over the long term. They pay out a guaranteed sum plus profits on maturity and are the most expensive form of life insurance. However, they are the only type of life insurance which can truly be classed as a savings vehicle. The policies commonly run for either 10 or 25 years.

So where is your money invested? After the insurance company has taken enough money from the premium to cover its costs and has made provision for death benefit in the event of the life assured dying before the policy matures, the rest of the premium is invested in the company's long-term fund. It is this fund which will provide the sum to be paid out on maturity. The fund is invested in a wide spread of different types of assets which might include cash deposits, loan stocks, government stocks (or 'gilts'), equities and property. The fund would aim not to be over-invested in any one sector so that if the performance of that sector was poor the fund's overall value would not suffer too much. Such a spread of investments should ensure a relatively safe, steady return on your money in the long term.

At maturity, a with-profits endowment policy pays out a guaranteed sum plus profits, which are added to the policy in the form of two types of bonus: reversionary and terminal. The size of the bonuses depends on the amount of profits made by the insurance company.

The reversionary bonus is added to the policy each year and is based on the sum assured. For example, if the sum assured is £1000 and a 4 per cent reversionary bonus is added each year, then at the end of year 1 the guaranteed sum will be £1000 + £40 and at the end of year 2 the bonus is added to the new guaranteed sum (i.e. £1040 + £41.60). It is important to note that once the reversionary bonus has been added to your policy the insurance company cannot later withdraw it.

The level of the reversionary bonus doesn't always reflect the level of the insurance company's profits in that particular year. If profits are especially high in one year, the company may decide to retain some of them so that it can at least maintain the level of bonuses in a lean year. As far as I know, there has never been a case of a life insurance company reducing its reversionary bonus rate.

Terminal bonuses are paid out on maturity of the policy and reflect the success of the insurance company's investments over the life of the policy. Unlike reversionary bonuses, terminal bonuses have been cut when insurance companies have shown a poor profit performance. However, they act as a very good incentive to hold your policy until maturity in order to get the maximum return on your money.

Exhibit 9.3 provides an illustration of the final pay-out for a man, now aged 54, who took out a with-profits endowment policy 25 years ago at an annual premium of £100.

Flexible endowment policies

Essentially these are with-profits endowment policies, which commonly run for ten-year periods, plus an

Exhibit 9.3 Illustration of the final pay-out on a with-profits endowment policy

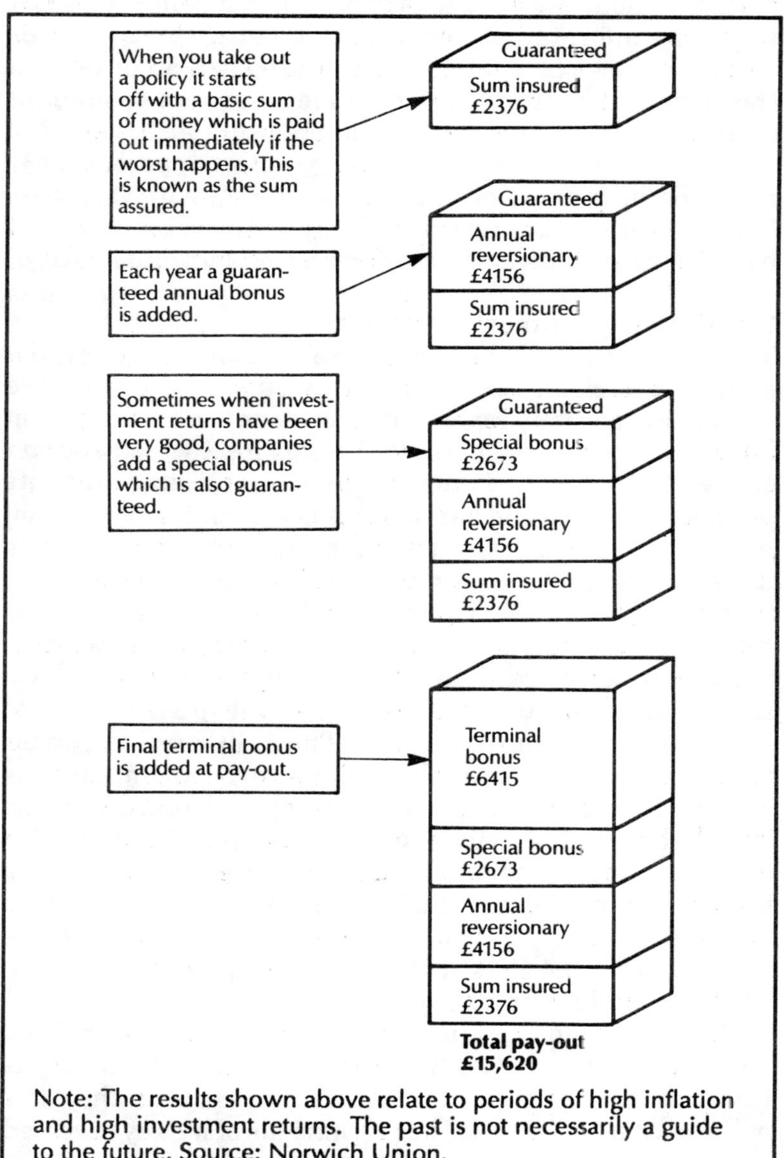

Note: The results shown above relate to periods of high inflation and high investment returns. The past is not necessarily a guide to the future. Source: Norwich Union.

additional feature: at the end of the first saving period you have a valuable option to start a second plan for a similar period without the need to provide the insurance company with any information about your health. However, this option may not be available if you are aged 55 or over at the start of the second period. Some insurance companies offer the option of increasing the premium at the start of the second term, which will give you the opportunity to raise the proportion of your saving in line with inflation. Because these plans are more flexible, the return will not be quite as good as a straightforward with-profits policy.

Unit-linked endowment life policies

These policies work in a completely different way to the policies described earlier in this section. Instead of the insurance company investing your money in its long-term fund, it usually offers a range of funds from which you can choose. Put simply, the insurance company distributes its profit by dividing the various funds into units. When you pay your premium, part of it will be used to purchase units in one of the funds. As the fund makes a profit and therefore grows, the value of each unit grows proportionately. This means that unlike non-unit linked policies, profit is *automatically* passed on to policy holders. Units are allocated to investors' policies at the 'offer price' and are encashed at the 'bid price'. The offer price is higher than the bid price and the difference between them is commonly called the spread. This spread represents an initial charge of usually five or six per cent. There is also an annual management charge taken from funds to cover the cost of managing the investments – typically, this totals about one per cent per annum of the value of the fund. Exhibit 9.4 lists just a few examples of sectors in which individual funds specialise.

Managed funds, as shown in the exhibit, invest in fixed interest stocks, equities, property and cash. The theory is that the managers switch into the investment they feel will perform best and so the proportions of money invested in each sector can vary enormously, unlike with the long-

Exhibit 9.4 Fund specialisation – sector examples

Fund	*Investments*
Deposit	Cash and near-cash short-term assets
Gilt-edged	UK government securities
Managed	Shares, property and fixed-interest stocks and cash
Index-linked	Index-linked stocks (predominantly gilts)
UK equity	UK ordinary shares and stocks convertible into shares
Far East equity	Japanese, Australian, Malaysian etc. ordinary shares
North American equity	US and Canadian shares
International equity	Geographically diversified share portfolio

term funds used by the non-unit linked companies. Therefore the unit-linked managed funds tend to carry more risk as do the other specialist equity and property funds.

The prices of units fluctuate all the time and you can follow movements in the financial sections of many newspapers and in the *Financial Times*. Clearly the value of units can go down as well as up and this makes unit-linked investment unsuitable for people who are not prepared to see the value of their hard-earned savings reduced. It is a suitable investment for people who do not mind the price fluctuations and who like to take an active interest in their investment. It is even possible to have a say in which fund your money is invested – you can switch into any of the other funds run by your company.

Why unit-linking? At first sight unit-linking may appear a relatively risky investment but, in fact, this is less true than it seems, especially when you understand the philosophy of the unit-linked insurance companies.

Basically, they believe that the major problem facing investors today is that of protecting the real value of their money against inflation. They also believe that the ideal long-term investments to make in order to beat inflation are in asset-backed vehicles such as shares and property. The types of funds that these companies have on offer reflect this philosophy. Asset-backed investments can be said to have two characteristics: first, they have the capacity to protect the real value of capital against inflation over the long term; and secondly, they carry the risk of a fall in value, particularly in the short term.

Please note that I have been stressing that unit-linked plans should only be considered for long-term investment and this means a minimum of 10 years but preferably longer than 15 years. There is plenty of reliable evidence demonstrating that over such a period asset-backed investments do keep pace with inflation and can beat it. Also, putting money into asset-backed investments at regular intervals introduces a notable feature called 'pound cost averaging' – the result of investing regularly is to even out price fluctuations.

Pound cost averaging. If you invest a fixed sum in units every month you will find that the average cost of the units will be below the average price for any given period. This is because the fixed sum buys more units in a month when prices are low and less units when prices are high. Exhibit 9.5 illustrates this using an exaggerated example based on £20 invested each month. As you can see, pound cost averaging irons out the effects of extreme

Exhibit 9.5 Pound cost averaging

Purchase date	*Unit offer price*	*Units purchased*
Month 1	500p	4
Month 2	250p	8
Month 3	400p	5
Average offer price	383p	

Total cost £60; total units purchased 17; average cost per unit equals 353p.

price fluctuations, bringing more stability to your investment.

Types of unit-linked plans. There are basically three types of plans available:

1. High investment plans;
2. High life cover plans; and
3. Balanced plans.

High investment plans provide minimal life cover in order to qualify as life assurance policies and invest most of your premium into units. The sort of life cover you might expect would be about 90 times your monthly premium. These plans make an excellent home for your long-term savings.

High life cover plans provide a very high level of life cover over a very long period of time for a minimal lifelong contribution. They are the unit-linked equivalent of a whole life policy. The term of these policies usually extends from 10 to 25 years but you can carry on your contributions for life. Just a very small part of your premium is invested in units and because of this the cash-in value of your plan will almost certainly be less than your contributions after 10 years – but, after 25 years, you might expect to double your money. This works out as a very poor investment, but a very cheap way of obtaining high life cover over a long period of time.

Balanced plans fall somewhere between high investment and high life cover plans. They offer a reasonable level of life cover from the start, although their investment performance is poor in the first 10 years. The return improves dramatically from year 10 onwards and this type of unit-linked policy is well suited to repaying a mortgage.

In addition, there are flexible unit-linked plans which allow you to choose or switch between any of these three types of plan, or to construct combinations within a single plan in order to provide the life insurance and investment elements you require. This, at first, seems very appealing, but it is best to keep your investment plans separate from your insurance plans so that should you need to cash in your plan unexpectedly to raise money, you can do so without affecting your life insurance. If you had to start another life policy you would be older, and premiums would be more expensive for the same cover. Also your health may have deteriorated.

Modern unit-linked policies are very flexible. Many offer an index-linked assurance option which allows the guaranteed sum assured to increase each year in line with inflation, or by a set percentage. When this option is exercised an additional contribution will be required to pay for the increase in life cover. The advantage of this is that the real value of your death benefits can be maintained without having to take out additional policies. The high investment plans often have an indexed contribution option, enabling your contributions to be increased in line with inflation so that your savings maintain their real value. These are very important facilities.

WHAT IF YOU CAN'T AFFORD THE PREMIUMS?

Another useful feature incorporated in many unit-linked policies is a waiver of contributions. For an additional two to six per cent of your premium, your regular premium can be waived if you are unable, through sickness or accident, to earn a living from your usual job for more than three months. This can act as a useful safeguard to your financial planning.

If you do not fall into this 'sickness or accident' category, with term insurance the position is clear – if you stop your payments you will lose your life cover. There is no surrender value with term insurance.

With endowment and unit-linked policies you have several options. First, you can surrender the policy which means that the insurance company will pay a cash sum in return for the policy. But as we have already seen, the surrender value during the early years will be extremely low and there is certainly no guarantee that an investor will receive back the money he or she has invested. In fact you are unlikely to receive anything if you surrender your policy within the first two years.

Another alternative is to take out a loan (from the insurance company itself) against the surrender value of the policy. This could be one way of continuing the premium payments through hard times. Up to 90 per cent of the surrender value can be borrowed and the capital is repaid from the policy proceeds on maturity. If you have been paying premiums for a considerable time this option is well worth considering. Also, if your policy has a cash-in value of at least £1000, you may be able to sell it in an auction. Whoever buys the policy carries on paying the premiums and collects the proceeds on maturity. There are a few firms (based in London) which auction policies.

If it is impossible to meet the premiums, but a cash sum is not required, then the policy can be converted into a paid-up policy. No more premiums will be due and the policy will mature on its due date. With unit-linked plans you may find that the plan has to be in force for a set period, say 4 years, and have a minimum cash-in value, typically £1000. This cash value can then be used to maintain life cover until the policy reserve is exhausted. This option at least continues to supply an element of important life cover. With non-unit linked policies the insurance company reduces the guaranteed sum for which you are insured to the paid-up value. In the case of with-profits plans, some companies will continue to add bonuses until maturity.

TAXATION

Subject to the exception described below, the proceeds of all qualifying life insurance policies are totally free of all income and capital gains tax in the hands of the investor. This makes life insurance policies particularly attractive to all taxpayers and especially to higher-rate taxpayers. The exception applies if a policy is surrendered or if premium payments cease within 10 years from inception, or the date of any variation. In such cases there may be a charge to income tax if your income at that time, including any chargeable gain under the plan, makes you liable to higher-rate tax. This proviso to tax exemption arises from the rules laid down for qualifying life policies, which include the requirement that premiums have to be paid annually or more frequently, and must be payable for a minimum of 10 years, except in the case of term policies.

Prior to 13th March, 1984, life insurance premiums were eligible for tax relief amounting to 15 per cent of the premium on a qualifying policy. If you took out a policy prior to this date and it is still in force you should still be getting tax relief but at a slightly reduced (although still valuable) rate of 12.5 per cent. There is no relief available on policies taken out after 13th March, 1984.

PROFITING FROM LIFE INSURANCE SAVINGS PLANS

Having discussed the basic types of life insurance policies available, we are now in a position to profit from our knowledge. First, you must of course already have an established emergency fund to meet any possible short-term needs before even contemplating life insurance savings plans. It bears repeating that a life insurance plan is a long-term investment, and if you cash in your plan early you can actually lose money. So make absolutely sure that, barring a major stroke of bad luck, you can easily afford the premiums over a very long period.

Having established this, the best type of life insurance policies to look at are with-profits endowment policies and unit-linked high investment plans. The minimum investment for a with-profits endowment policy can be as little as £4 per month, which over a full year works out at less than 93 pence per week. Unit-linked plans can start from as little as £10 per month but more usually the minimum is set at around £25 per month.

The next thing to do is to pick an insurance company that will give you the best return on your money. *Money Management* magazine occasionally publishes surveys showing the performances of various insurance companies' with-profits endowment policies. The difference in performance between the best and the worst is considerable so you should not only pick the type of plan to suit your needs but also pick a company showing consistently above-average performance. Another source of such information is *Planned Savings*. For unit-linked plans you can compare the performance of the insurance bond funds, but be sure and look at the 10-year performance figures. These comparisons can be found in *Money Management* each month.

As a very rough idea of what to expect back from your investment, a man aged under 30 at the outset of taking out a 10-year with-profits endowment plan might expect to double his money, and on a 25-year plan could receive back 4 times the total premiums paid in. These are average figures taken from a survey of £30 per month level contribution plans. The survey showed that the top companies performed significantly better. So saving a regular sum of money, which in the short term you probably won't miss, can make you significantly better off in the long term.

Exhibit 9.6 illustrates the return on a savings plan on two bases: 7 per cent per annum and 10.5 per cent per annum. The illustration is set out in accordance with LAUTRO rules and therefore the returns do not necessarily represent what you will actually receive. In fact, if you compare the figures for £50 per month with the actual return for this particular plan (based on a 1978 start date and cashed at maturity 10 years later), the actual return was considerably better than the LAUTRO figures. The latter therefore cannot be used as a basis for comparing similar policies, but, as illustrative figures, they will provide you with some idea of what different growth rates mean in practice.

£50 per month works out at just £1.65 per day and it is astonishing to think that you could turn this into over £11,700 in just 10 years. Society's attitude tends to be that regular saving is boring. Waking up one morning to find a

Exhibit 9.6 Life insurance savings plans – an illustration

Illustration
A male non-smoker aged 30 next birthday.

Contribution
£50 monthly, payable by direct debit.

Guaranteed death benefit
£4500 or, if greater, the bid value of the units.

Future benefits
On alternative assumptions of the rate of growth in the unit prices of accumulation units (7% p.a., basis 1; 10.5% p.a., basis 2), cash values resulting from contributions are:

	Cash values (£s)		
Years in force	*Basis 1*	*Basis 2*	*Total outlay*
5	3031	3283	3000
6	3828	4224	3600
7	4679	5261	4200
8	5589	6406	4800
9	6560	7669	5400
10	7597	9061	6000

Historical benefits
Benefits after 10 years for a male non-smoker, now aged 39, who started a plan in 1978:

Monthly investment	*Guaranteed life cover*	*Cash sum payable*
£20	2031.00	4591.17
£30	3078.00	6957.88
£50	5172.00	11691.35
£75	7790.00	17609.29

Source: Guardian Royal Exchange.

cheque for £11,700 on the doormat does not fit my definition of boring – nor, I suspect, most other people's.

PLANNING FOR MAJOR PURCHASES

The best time to start saving is when you are young because the premiums are cheaper for the same guaranteed sum assured and, of course, there is so much to save for. It could be a smart new car or a deposit on a house – the list is endless. The point is, with-profits endowment savings schemes allow you to plan for major purchases.

For instance, say you enjoy sailing and at present you are happy to borrow or hire boats for the odd weekend while you become more expert. In a few years hence you foresee having more time to devote to your hobby, at which point you would dearly like to have your own yacht – price tag: £10,000. Why not take out a 10-year with-profits endowment plan with a sum assured of around the same amount. This would ensure that you would be able to buy your yacht in 10-years time and the bonuses added to your sum assured would help to reduce the effects of inflation. So although prices go up each year you will still be able to afford the yacht when your policy matures. The premiums may seem quite high to start with, but when you are young with few commitments it is an ideal time to save for something worthwhile and after a few years, inflation will start to erode the value of your premiums and it will not seem so bad.

Another way of achieving the same ends is to take out a low-start policy under which the premiums increase steadily each year. Some policies enable you to increase your premiums for each of the first five years while others, particularly unit-linked plans, give you the option to increase your premium in line with inflation. This helps maintain the real value of your savings and also means that if you expect your earnings to increase over the years you should be able to afford the increases in premium and secure a better return at the end of the term.

Exhibits 9.7 and 9.8 illustrate the benefits under level-contribution and low-start with-profits endowment policies respectively. Exhibit 9.7 sets out the case of a £10 per month level contribution over 35 years. Again this illustration complies with the LAUTRO rules and actual performance may well be better, especially over a long period such as this. £10 per month works out at just 33

Exhibit 9.7 An illustration of a level-contribution, with-profits endowment policy

Illustration
A male, aged less than 30, for a term of 35 years.

Cost
Monthly premium £10; maximum total outlay £4200.

Guaranteed benefits
On survival to the end of the term, or on earlier death: £3946

Future benefits
Benefits at the end of the term (including guaranteed benefits): Basis 1, £13,500; Basis 2, £29,200. (Bases 1 and 2 assume rates of return of 7% and 10.5% p.a. in accordance with the LAUTRO requirements.)

Source: Guardian Royal Exchange.

pence per day, but look at the sum of money a 30-year-old could expect to receive when he retires at 65.

The monthly premium on the low-start policy illustrated in Exhibit 9.8 begins at £10 per month and increases on each of the first 4 policy anniversaries up to a maximum of £20 per month. Comparing this with the level-contribution illustration of £10 per month (Exhibit 9.7) the difference in future benefits over 35 years is remarkable.

A further way of using with-profits endowment plans is to take out a new level premium plan regularly (every year if possible, or at least every five years). This means that you will have policies maturing at regular intervals producing either tax-free additional income or a lump sum. You could use this system as a self-financing savings scheme by re-investing these pay-outs in a series of new plans, or you might adapt it to provide a method of financing school fees.

REPAYING THE MORTGAGE

With-profits endowment plans are used extensively as a means of paying off mortgages. You pay interest to your

Exhibit 9.8 An illustration of a low-start, with-profits endowment policy

Illustration
A male, aged less than 30, for a term of 35 years.

Cost
Monthly premium payable in the first year £10.00, increasing by £2.50 at each of the first four policy anniversaries; maximum total outlay £8100.

Guaranteed benefits
On survival to the end of the term, or on earlier death: £7040.

Future benefits
Benefits at the end of the term (including guaranteed benefits): Basis 1, £23,600; Basis 2, £51,000. (Bases 1 and 2 assume rates of return of 7% and 10.5% p.a., using an equivalent level monthly premium of £16.90, in accordance with the LAUTRO requirements.)

Source: Guardian Royal Exchange.

lender and pay a regular monthly premium into a plan which repays the loan on maturity, or earlier death.

One of the most popular types of policy is a low-cost endowment mortgage: the guaranteed death benefit ensures that the mortgage will be paid off on your death but the guaranteed endowment sum insured is set at a much lower level, relying on the bonuses added each year to make up the required sum on maturity. If the bonuses are poor there is no guarantee that the cash sum on maturity will be enough to repay your mortgage, although this is unlikely. A good performance will ensure that you will have paid for your house, and possibly have an additional cash sum as well.

The regular saver can therefore take advantage of an endowment mortgage as an opportunity to pay for a house and possibly save a substantial sum of money. If you can afford it you could take out a with-profits endowment plan with a guaranteed endowment sum assured equal to the sum borrowed (e.g. £40,000). This would guarantee the repayment of your mortgage at maturity and, with the additional bonuses, you would have a very sizeable tax-free lump sum at the end of the term.

Unit-linked plans are not as suitable as with-profits endowment plans for paying off, or saving for, a specific sum of money over a 10-year period because the return can fluctuate enormously in the final year prior to maturity. They are, however, much more suitable for the longer-term investment of 15 years and more, when they can out-perform with-profits plans by a considerable margin. They are also more flexible and a unit-linked mortgage plan is particularly well suited to paying off a 25-year mortgage. Even a poor performance will guarantee to pay off your mortgage, while a good performance will produce an extra substantial sum of money. Also, many plans enable you to pay off your loan early. It is best to use unit-linked savings plans if you do not need a specific sum of money at a particular date. If you plan to save for a period of 15 years or more they are probably the best type of plan available.

SUMMARY

Advantages

1. An excellent way for the regular saver to invest money over the long term.
2. Very small sums of money can be set aside monthly – often smaller minimums than for bank or building society savings schemes.
3. The additional valuable benefit of life cover should you die.
4. With certain plans your return can be guaranteed.
5. With unit-linked plans your money is invested in asset-backed investments such as shares and property, which over the long term have the capacity to protect savings against inflation.
6. For qualifying policies, returns at maturity are completely free of all income and capital gains tax in the hands of the investor. This makes them extremely

attractive for all taxpayers, especially high-rate taxpayers.

7. Many unit-linked plans are very flexible and allow you to increase your premiums in line with inflation to help maintain the real value of your contributions.
8. Your money is professionally managed. It is invested in a spread of investments so you do not have all your eggs in one basket.
9. You can use a policy to obtain a loan from the insurance company.
10. There is no maximum investment restriction.
11. Proceeds can often be taken as tax-free regular income.
12. The investment performance of these savings plans over the long term can be substantially better than putting your money in the bank or building society.

Disadvantages

1. Only suitable as a long-term investment.
2. Surrendering your policy early should be avoided as the cash value of your plan in the early years can be extremely low. You will be lucky to receive any of your money back if you surrender your policy within the first two years.
3. Early surrender could make you liable to higher-rate income tax on the proceeds.
4. Premiums become more expensive the older and less healthy you become.
5. Care must be taken when choosing your insurance company because investment performance varies considerably between the best and the worst performing companies.

To sum up therefore, savings-type insurance policies make an excellent home for your long-term savings, with the added benefit of life insurance. Before considering these plans you must make sure that you can easily afford the premiums. The insurance companies offer a very wide range of products to suit all sorts of needs. It's best to choose a well known company whose long-term performance has been above average. You can compare performances in publications such as *Planned Savings* and *Money Management*, copies of which should be available at your local library. If you write to insurance companies they will be only too pleased to supply information about their products and, if you wish, you can ask a representative to call.

Once invested, your money is professionally managed and is protected in law by the Policy Holders' Protection Act. At maturity the proceeds are tax free in the hands of the investor making this type of investment particularly attractive to higher-rate taxpayers.

It may seem a bit unexciting to save money over such a long period, but it will all be worthwhile when your cheque arrives on the doormat. It is an excellent way of planning for the future, it provides something to look forward to and, with patience, you really can build your fortune. Success comes to those who plan it and patience, in this case, will be well rewarded. In Part III I will look at how insurance policies can fit into your financial plans, helping you to make the best use of your resources and to solve some important financial problems.

10 Unit Trust Savings Plans

Unit trusts are ideally suited to regular investment over the long term. Like the unit-linked insurance plans we looked at in the last chapter, unit trusts provide a simple way for individuals to invest indirectly in the world's stockmarkets, although without, in this case, the costs or benefits of life insurance. They make it possible for a number of investors to pool their money to create a large enough fund to be spread over a wide range of companies and industries, either at home or abroad.

Unit trusts are run by the major investment management groups, many of which also offer unit trust savings plans with minimum investment levels set at about £25 per month. This means that individual investors, with quite small sums of money, can have access to the kind of investment power that was once considered the preserve of the rich. By pooling the savings of many individuals, the management groups produce a large sum which can then enjoy the benefits of professional investment expertise in the various stockmarkets of the world.

WHAT IS A UNIT TRUST?

A unit trust is a fund into which investors pool their money. This money is then invested by professional managers primarily into equities (i.e. company ordinary shares) although they may also invest in cash, government stocks ('gilts') or loan stocks. Authorised unit trusts (trusts approved by the Department of Trade and Industry), unlike insurance funds, are not allowed to invest directly in property or commodities.

When an investor contributes money to the fund, he or she receives a number of units, each reflecting the total value of the fund divided by the number of units in existence. Unit trusts are known as 'open-ended' funds because when new money is received by the managers new units are created. When investors want to withdraw their money, units are cancelled in exchange for cash.

Unit trusts are listed in the newspapers with two prices – investors buy units at the offer price which is the higher of the prices quoted; the lower figure is the bid price which is the price investors receive when they sell. The difference between the two prices (commonly called the 'spread') is usually about seven per cent. The significance of this to investors is that the price of units must rise by the amount of the spread before they can recoup their original investment. The purpose of the spread is to cover management costs such as administration, dealing and trustee expenses. The only other charge is an annual management fee, usually around one per cent, which is automatically deducted from the dividend income paid to unitholders.

Units come in two forms – distribution and accumulation units. If the trust is a distribution trust (the most common type), the dividend is paid in cash, net of basic-rate tax, normally once or twice a year. With accumulation units, the net income earned by the underlying investments is retained by the fund, and the end result is that the value of a single unitholder's investment increases in proportion to the income the fund has retained. The taxation treatment of unit trust investment is considered later in the chapter.

In the newspapers you will occasionally see the letters 'XD' shown next to the price of a trust, standing for ex distribution. A trust will go XD the day after its accounting day. Anyone buying units on this date, or during the following six weeks, will not receive the next distribution but, to compensate for this, the unit price falls.

TRUST OBJECTIVES

Unit trusts are divided into a number of different categories depending on their investment objectives and each management group has many different trusts, each with different aims. There are three basic categories: income trusts, growth trusts and balanced trusts.

Income trusts are usually designed for investors who need a reasonable level of income which has a chance of increasing over the years in line with inflation. The growth trusts' main objective is capital appreciation, which might be achieved through investment in smaller company shares, recovery situations or through specialisation in overseas countries. Balanced trusts will seek to provide a balance between income and capital growth. Some advice on how to go about choosing a unit trust is provided later on in the chapter.

WHO SUPERVISES YOUR INVESTMENT

Your investment is supervised by independent trustees. These are substantial financial institutions such as insurance companies and banks. The trustees must ensure that the investment aims of the trust are complied with and these aims are set out in the trust deed which, with all authorised unit trusts, must be approved by the Department of Trade and Industry.

Other tasks performed by the trustees include safeguarding unitholders' assets, collecting the trust's dividend income and distributing income to unitholders. The various roles of the trustees are designed to ensure that the managers are properly supervised.

Unauthorised trusts

You may encounter unauthorised unit trusts. These differ from authorised trusts in that the trust deed has not been formally approved by the DTI: unauthorised trusts cannot be advertised in the UK but details can be supplied on request. Although most of the funds are respectable, there may well be an additional risk element because there is no guarantee of independent trustees and there could be problems if a large number of investors decide to cash in their investment at the same time. One reason for this is that unauthorised trusts are allowed to invest directly in commodities and property (i.e. illiquid investments) which may prove difficult to sell under such pressing circumstances.

Offshore unit trusts also come under the unauthorised category and suitable ones may appeal to non-UK residents because of their potential tax benefits. As far as the UK investor is concerned, those based in the Channel Islands or the Isle of Man should be as secure as an authorised trust, provided the managers are UK clearing banks or another highly respectable institution. Other offshore funds could be risky because of the lack of supervision and they require a cautious approach.

HOW SAVINGS PLANS WORK

Most of the major unit trust management groups offer savings plans. You are invited to make regular monthly contributions, usually by standing order or direct debit, which are used to buy units in the fund of your choice at the offer price. The usual minimum subscription is £25 and there is no maximum. Although most groups insist that you invest on a monthly basis, there are a few schemes that will accept occasional additional payments. So if you have some spare cash you can make extra purchases under these schemes as long as the extra amounts themselves meet the applicable minimum. Initially your payments are invested in accumulation units, but if you need income then you can convert into distribution units provided your holding is £500 or more.

Unit trust savings plans are quite flexible because you can increase your contribution at any time, reduce it to the minimum or stop contributions altogether leaving your holding intact.

Sellers must give written instructions and receive the bid price ruling at the date the managers receive them. It usually takes about 10 days for your cheque to come through. It is also possible to switch your units into a different trust within the range offered by the management group.

Unit trust savings schemes should be regarded as a long-term, regular investment. As with all stockmarket-related investments, they carry a risk of a fall in value over the short term, but long-term performance is likely to protect the value of your money against inflation. As discussed in the 'Unit-linked endowment life policies' section in Chapter Nine, regular investment means you can take advantage of pound cost averaging, making fluctuations in the stockmarket work to your advantage. Exhibit 10.1 shows past performance figures compiled by the Unit Trust Association, indicating returns on a £30 per month investment across different time-scales.

CHOOSING UNIT TRUSTS

This is not easy because there are around 1000 individual funds to choose from and 170 or so different unit trust management groups. Many groups offer unit trust saving schemes so you really are spoilt for choice. But there are

Exhibit 10.1 Unit trust savings plan returns as at October 1989 (investing £30 per month)

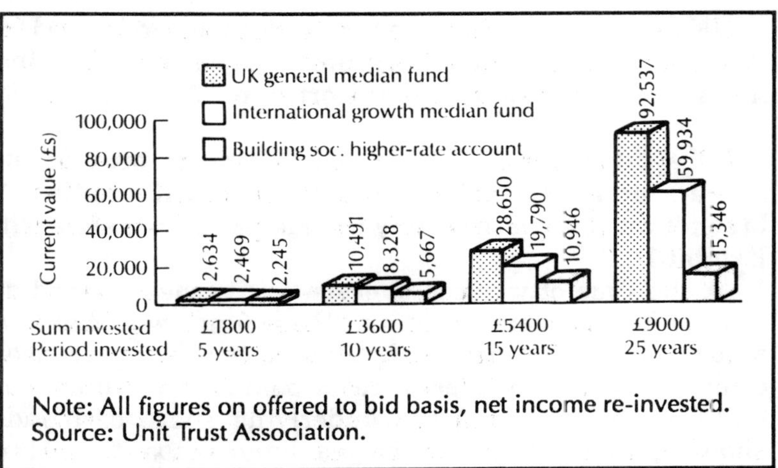

Note: All figures on offered to bid basis, net income re-invested.
Source: Unit Trust Association.

some guidelines for trust selection which you may find helpful.

STAGE ONE – BEFORE YOU START

Make sure that unit trust investment is appropriate for you. As I mentioned earlier, unit trusts must be viewed as a long-term investment from the outset, despite the fact that it is possible to make considerable short-term gains. It is important that you have an adequate emergency fund readily available because unit trust prices fluctuate downwards as well as upwards and, as an investor, you should be in a position to choose the moment when you sell, rather than be forced to sell when the market may be temporarily depressed. Your emergency fund should save you from being a forced seller.

STAGE TWO – YOUR PERSONAL OBJECTIVES

Try to pick a trust that best suits your objectives. Your starting point should be to look at the various trust categories.

UK general. These funds invest in the UK to provide a balance between income and capital growth.

UK growth. Again these funds are invested in the UK but their main aim is capital growth. Any income from the investments is of secondary importance.

UK equity income. These trusts aim to provide an above average income from a portfolio of UK equities. A breakdown of a typical equity income portfolio is shown in Exhibit 10.2.

At the time of writing, average equity yields stand at around four per cent gross, and these funds would aim to secure about five per cent. This may seem very poor compared with the interest rates paid by the banks and building societies, but the underlying share dividends should grow steadily over the years and so too should the yield on your original investment, rather than fluctuating

Exhibit 10.2 UK equity income fund – portfolio analysis

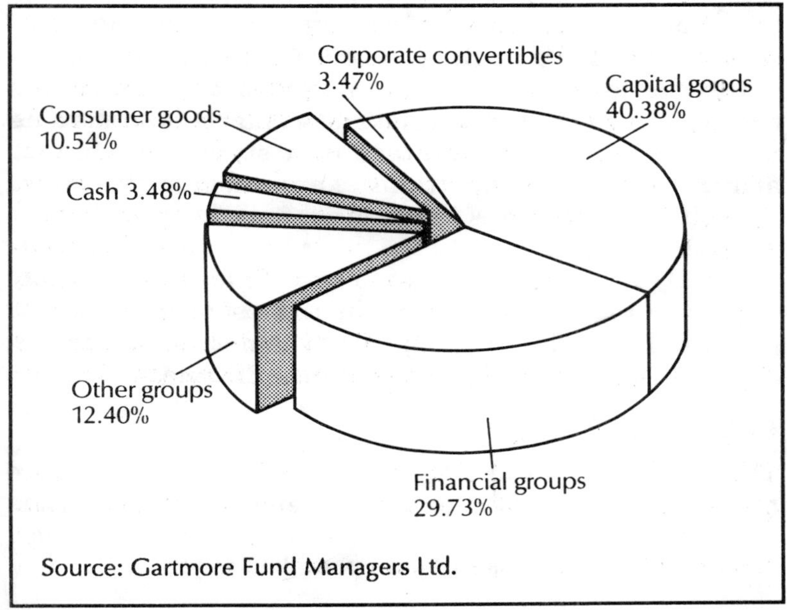

Source: Gartmore Fund Managers Ltd.

in line with interest rates. Also, the portfolio's ability to produce a higher income should be reflected in a higher value for the fund and so this type of trust should also achieve good capital growth over the long term.

Mixed income. Mixed income trusts aim for even higher income by investing in preference shares and gilts with just a small proportion of their assets being invested in ordinary shares. The total return for these funds (i.e. including capital appreciation) is usually much lower than for equity income funds.

Gilt and fixed interest. These trusts aim to achieve a very high income (say 10 per cent gross) but there is very little room for capital growth, and I believe that if you want to buy gilts for income you would be best advised to hold them directly.

Other categories. These include trusts which specialise in investing in shares in particular sectors (e.g. investment trust, commodity/energy, financial and property shares). Their main concern is for capital growth.

International trusts seek a spread of investments throughout all the world's major stockmarkets so that the managers can take advantage of a strong economy or attractive currency opportunities anywhere in the world. Exhibit 10.3 illustrates the composition of a typical international fund.

Finally, some trusts invest in specific markets or geographical areas, and their main aim is usually capital growth. Examples include North America, Australia, Japan, the Far East, Europe and Scandinavia.

STAGE THREE – RISK

The next thing to decide is what level of risk you are prepared to take. This is a very personal thing – some

Exhibit 10.3 Global equity fund – portfolio analysis

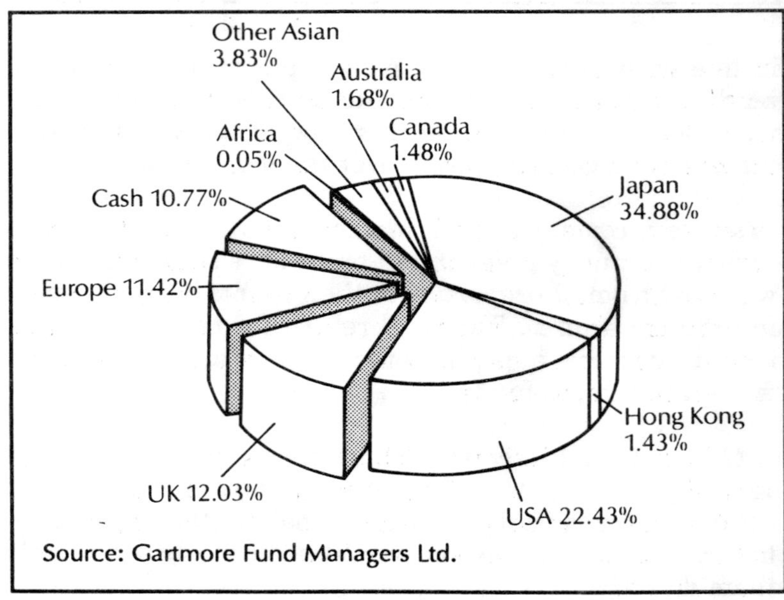

Source: Gartmore Fund Managers Ltd.

people prefer caution, others enjoy a 'flutter'. Whatever your disposition, there is almost certainly a unit trust to suit.

One of the more cautious types of trust is the UK equity income. These tend to invest in shares likely to give an increasing income over the years. If you look after the income you can leave the capital growth to look after itself. A UK fund investing a higher proportion of its assets in gilts or preference shares may be less risky but the growth record is likely to be less favourable over the long term. A fund investing mostly in smaller companies may carry greater risk but could well be suitable for those prepared to accept more risk in return for potentially higher rewards. Trusts that invest in specific sectors such as property or gold shares are usually very high risk. They are very much like putting all your eggs in one basket and are best suited to the experienced and the brave.

The same cannot be said of the international funds which own a spread of equities in a spread of markets. However, the additional risk for these funds (relative to those invested solely in the UK) is that of exposure to currency fluctuations which can wipe out spectacular investment gains. Although many of the international funds are solid, if unspectacular performers, for more specialised funds (e.g. those investing in only one country) currency movements can make a huge difference to investment returns when they are translated into sterling terms. Some managers try to neutralise currency effects by hedging but this is not always easy.

Although trusts investing overseas may be risky, they do provide an opportunity for considerable gains. But a word of warning when investing in trusts that specialise in less developed countries or emerging economies: you must bear in mind the additional possibility of political instability which may be an extra risk you are not prepared to take.

Another factor which affects a fund's risk rating is its size. In theory a small fund should be able to respond more quickly than a large one to changing market conditions. In reality there is little evidence to support this. On the other hand, it is unlikely that you will find a large fund at the top, or at the bottom, of its performance table and, therefore, if you are only prepared to take an average risk in the category you choose, pick a large fund. It is worth adding that some management groups use one of their smaller funds as a flagship in which they place their favoured investments so that similar funds in the same sector can be marketed to investors on the basis of the flagship's performance.

To help you ascertain which funds are high and low risk, some management groups number their trusts. Number one would represent a very low-risk trust, while higher numbers indicate increasing risk. If you are considering investing in a unit trust savings scheme for the first time, my advice is that you restrict yourself to either a UK or an international trust. If the amount you have to invest each month is high enough, you may consider splitting the total between a high-risk and low-risk trust, or dividing the money between different management groups.

STAGE FOUR – CHOOSING A MANAGEMENT GROUP

The only guideline you have to go on here is past performance. You need to pick a group which has consistently performed well over the longer term – a single year of growth may be 'a flash in the pan'. A readily available source of information on unit trust performance is *Money Management*, a monthly magazine which contains performance tables covering periods up to 10 years.

Past performance, however, is going to be of little use when you are considering investing in a brand new trust. These new trusts are carefully researched and, with a fresh pool of cash, are launched when the managers feel that market conditions are most favourable. To encourage new investors the managers sometimes reduce the front-end loading charge, thereby offering more units for your money. If market conditions do indeed turn out to be favourable, investing in a new trust can prove very profitable.

Once you have chosen a unit trust, the mechanics of investing are simple – it is just a case of filling in an application form and sending it off with a cheque for the first monthly instalment.

Once or twice a year you will receive a statement showing how many units you have bought and at what price, and you will be able to work out the up-to-date value of your investment by looking up the price in, for example, the *Financial Times*. An example of the usual statement format is shown in Exhibit 10.4. It is based on an investor paying £20 per month, as recorded in column two. Column one shows the date of the investment and column three the purchase price of units. Column four records how many units were purchased in each transaction, with the run-

Exhibit 10.4 Unit trust savings plan statement

Item and date	*Cash rec'd or paid*	*Price per unit*	*Units bought/sold*	*Total holding*
Balance (16/09)			4219.7177	4219.7177
Purchase (26/09)	£20.00	81.37p	24.5791	4244.2968
Purchase (26/10)	£20.00	86.05p	23.2423	4267.5391
Purchase (28/11)	£20.00	83.26p	24.0211	4291.5602
Purchase (28/12)	£20.00	81.90p	24.4200	4315.9802
Purchase (26/01)	£20.00	89.25p	22.4090	4338.3892
Purchase (27/02)	£20.00	90.49p	22.1019	4360.4911
Distribution (17/03)	£49.50	95.88p	51.6270	4412.1181

For the period covered by this statement, £169.50 was invested into your savings plan account. On 20th March this account had a value of £3891.93 using a bid price of 88.21p.

Source: Barclays Unicorn Group Limited.

ning total consolidated in column five. The figure of £49.50 in column two is a distribution payment which was re-invested back into the plan.

TAXATION

As discussed earlier, dividends from distribution trusts are paid in cash. This payment is net of basic-rate tax and a voucher indicating the amount of tax deducted is attached to dividend cheques. Therefore a basic-rate taxpayer has no further liability but, unlike bank or building society interest, non-taxpayers can reclaim the tax deducted. When you look in the paper to see what dividend is paid you will note that yields are quoted on a gross basis, before deducting tax, so a yield of 10 per cent gross is equivalent to 7.5 per cent net of basic-rate tax, currently 25 per cent.

Holders of accumulation units (where the net income earned on the underlying investments is retained by the fund) still receive a tax credit voucher despite the fact that they do not actually see the income. It is an important document because it enables non-taxpayers to reclaim tax and higher-rate taxpayers to settle the balance with the Inland Revenue. Exhibit 10.5 provides an example of such a tax voucher (the one attached to the statement shown in Exhibit 10.4), detailing a tax credit of £16.28.

Gains made as a result of a sale of units are subject to capital gains tax, but there is little likelihood of actually having to pay tax, especially in the short term, because of the current annual exemption. Even in the longer term, any tax payable will probably be minimal because of the indexation allowance as well as the annual exemption.

UNIT TRUST TERMINOLOGY

Before reviewing the advantages and disadvantages of unit trust savings schemes, it may be helpful to briefly consolidate in a glossary some of the main items of unit trust terminology.

Exhibit 10.5 Tax credit voucher

Distribution
Details of the distribution for the period 6th August, 1989 to 1st February 1990, due 2nd April, 1990.

Account	*Acct.No.*	*Units held*	*Tax credit*
Savings	14046/5/33	4338.3892	£16.28

Account	*Payable per unit*	*Income distribution*	*Equalisation*	*Amount due*
Savings	1.1408p	£48.82	£0.68	£49.50

We certify that advance corporation tax equal to the total of the amount(s) shown above as a Tax Credit will be accounted for to the Collector of Taxes.

Yours faithfully,
THE MANAGERS

Source: Barclays Unicorn (Trustees) Limited.

Accumulation units. With these units, income is not paid out to you direct but is retained by the fund and is reflected in the unit price.

Bid price. The lower of the two prices quoted and the price the investor receives on selling units.

Distribution units. Units entitling the holder to receive regular income payments in cash.

Equities. Another word for ordinary shares.

Gilts. UK government stocks.

Gross yield. Annual income from the unit trust investment, expressed as a percentage of the offer price before deduction of tax.

Hedging. A method of neutralising the effects of movements in currency values.

Managers. The people who look after your investment and take the important investment decisions.

Offer price. The higher of the two prices quoted and the one at which the investor buys units.

Portfolio. The complete list of a fund's investments.

Preference shares. Shares which rank before ordinary shares on the liquidation of a company. The maximum dividend on preference shares is fixed and they carry less risk than ordinary shares.

Spread. The difference between the bid and offer prices.

Tax voucher. Investors should retain this for filling in their tax returns because it shows the Inland Revenue the income tax that has already been paid.

Trustees. Trustees are independent of the investment managers and they ensure that the investment aims of the trust, and other requirements, are complied with.

XD. Ex distribution. If you buy units when they are marked 'XD' you are not entitled to receive the next income payment.

SUMMARY

Advantages

1. An excellent method of saving over the long term.
2. Less costly in the early years than unit-linked insurance plans.
3. An indirect investment in a diversified portfolio enjoying the benefits of professional investment expertise for as little as £25 per month.
4. A way of investing indirectly in overseas stock-markets.
5. The savings plans have enormous flexibility without penalty. You can get at your money normally within two weeks.
6. Dividends are paid net of basic-rate tax but the tax can be reclaimed by non-taxpayers. This makes the plans suitable for children, and accounts for under-14s can be opened in the name of an adult and designated with the child's full name.
7. The value of your savings is likely to keep pace with inflation over the long term and possibly beat it.

8. Unlike insurance funds, unit trusts themselves (as opposed to unitholders) are entirely free from capital gains tax, which means that the managers can buy and sell shares on their investment merits alone. This can result in a better return from your investment.
9. There is no maximum investment restriction.

Disadvantages

1. Only suitable as a long-term investment.
2. Gains are subject to capital gains tax in the hands of the investor.
3. The value of your investment can go down as well as up, especially in the short term.
4. It can be difficult to decide which unit trust group to choose and, then, which of their trusts you should invest in.
5. Under very extreme stockmarket conditions it may be difficult to sell your units.
6. There are no life insurance benefits.

Unit trust savings plans provide an excellent way to accumulate very substantial sums over the longer term. They should certainly be considered once you have taken care of your emergency, medium-term and insurance needs and they provide an ideal method of indirect stockmarket investment. Because these plans do not provide life insurance cover, they do not incur the associated costs and are therefore very much more flexible – there are no penalties for withdrawals in the early years.

One of the main advantages of unit trusts is that they invest primarily in shares of companies operating in different commercial and industrial fields. They can, therefore, share in the valuable rewards of investing in successful businesses. Over the long term it is only likely to be this sort of performance which will beat inflation. Careful share selection is needed and it is important that you pick a successful unit trust management group with a consistently good, long-term record. To help you decide, look at the performance tables in *Money Management*.

This sort of investment is inappropriate for those who are not prepared to see the value of their savings fall in the short term and who worry about fluctuations in the price of their units. For others, however, saving £25 a month over a period of 10–15 years in one of these plans can prove extremely worthwhile.

11 Investment Trust Savings Schemes

These schemes have only been available since 1984 and, although they have generated quite a lot of interest from long-term savers, it is fair to say that their usefulness is not widely appreciated. There are several reasons for this. First, there are strict advertising rules that investment trusts have to abide by and, secondly, unlike other savings products, there are no highly paid sales people to promote investment trust savings plans. So what are investment trusts and how do they differ from unit trusts?

INVESTMENT TRUSTS

Investment trusts are similar to unit trusts in that both consist of a spread of professionally managed investments. This aside, however, there are some important differences between the two types of trust.

Investment trusts are public limited companies with a fixed share capital and their shares are listed on the stock exchange. They can therefore be bought and sold by stockbrokers acting for investors. An investment trust is a 'closed-ended' fund: hence, unlike with unit trusts, the purchase or sale of an investment trust's shares does not result in cash payments to and from the managers or into and out of the trust. An investment trust has a fixed capital to invest and can therefore plan its strategy and organisation on a long-term basis, taking a long-term view of the underlying investments without having to worry about short-term performance. In extreme cases when there are a lot of investors wanting to withdraw their funds from a unit trust, the managers may have to cash in an investment at a loss to meet the demand for redemptions. In the Crash of 1987 the majority of unit trusts were unable to quote a price, or deal for many days, whereas with investment trusts you could get a quote from your broker and sell your holding without difficulty.

An investment trust's capital is invested in shares (quoted, unquoted, domestic and foreign) and these securities comprise the bulk of a trust's assets. You will often find that the price of an investment trust's shares is at a considerable discount to its underlying net asset value (i.e. the value of its investment portfolio) – typically, around 20 per cent. Unlike unit trusts, the price of an investment trust is not laid down by any formula but, in the same way as other shares, depends on market forces. Therefore, the discount can vary. An investor who buys an investment trust's shares in effect acquires a broad range of professionally managed investments through that single shareholding. It is possible to follow the ups and downs in performance because investment trust share prices are quoted in most of the newspapers.

THE DISCOUNT

As I have mentioned, share prices are set by market forces, and with most investment trusts the share price is generally below the underlying net asset value. This discount is calculated as follows: net asset value, less the share price times 100, divided by the net asset value. For example, if an investment trust's share price is currently 160p and its net asset value is 200p the discount is 20 per cent.

But why are most investment trusts priced at a discount? First, if the trust was to liquidate itself (i.e. sell its entire portfolio), it may not be able to secure the quoted value for the shares, especially those that are difficult to deal in and those in which it has a large holding. There are also selling costs to consider. Another factor is that many investment trusts are too small to attract institutional investors and therefore demand for the shares is less than you might otherwise expect. As a result investors generally expect to see investment trust shares trading at a discount and if the discount seems too small then a fall in demand for the shares will tend to depress the price and increase the discount; conversely, if the discount seems too large, demand for the shares will tend to push the price upwards, reducing the discount.

The effect of the discount is twofold. Firstly, discounts tend to narrow in a rising market and widen in a falling market. Therefore as the net asset value rises the share price will rise even more as the discount narrows. This is fine in a rising market, but it works the other way in a falling market. This makes investment trusts a more interesting and exciting investment for many people.

Secondly, a discount means that the investor earns income on more assets than he actually pays for. For example, suppose an investor buys 1000 shares in an investment trust when the price is 200p and the net asset value is 240p. The total cost to the investor (see Exhibit 11.1) is £2043 which means, in other words, that £2043 acquires £2400 worth of assets.

Compare this with buying a unit trust, where if you invested £2043 you would expect to obtain assets worth £1900 (£2043 less the 7 per cent spread). In theory then, the same amount of money should generate more income from investment in an investment trust than would be received from a unit trust.

As you can see, the discount adds some interesting elements to your investment. A factor adding further spice

Exhibit 11.1 The cost of buying 1000 investment trust shares at 200p per share

Item	*Cost (£s)*
Purchase consideration (1000 x 200p)	2000
Brokerage commission at 1.65 per cent	33
Stamp duty	10
Total cost of shares	2043

is that investment trusts can borrow money in just the same way as any other limited company, and this is one method they have to increase their assets. Unit trusts cannot do this. Also, investment trusts can offset the interest cost against tax which individuals cannot do if they borrow to invest in stocks and shares.

HOW THE PLANS WORK

Investment trust savings schemes offer a very simple and cost effective way of building up a shareholding in a trust, and like other equity-based investments should be considered as a long-term investment. You can make regular monthly payments of as little as £20 per month, and with most schemes there is a designated dealing day each month when your money is used to buy as many shares as possible in the investment trust. Investors receive the maximum number of whole shares their contribution will buy, less expenses. Any money not invested will be carried forward to next month's total.

The first thing to note about these schemes is that because very large sums of money are invested once a month on behalf of savers, the trust companies can negotiate very low commission rates with their brokers, commonly 0.2–1.0 per cent, plus stamp duty. Although some companies impose their own administration charges it still works out considerably cheaper than going direct to a stockbroker who would normally charge 1.65 per cent. These low charges give investment trusts an edge over their rival unit trusts – especially when added to the fact that the annual management fees also tend to be set at a lower level.

The second thing to note is that you must be careful about your investment timing. Most of the schemes invest just once a month, and if you time your investment on the wrong date you will have cash lying uninvested for possibly three or four weeks. You must therefore check which dates the share purchases are made, and plan your investments accordingly.

Exhibit 11.2 Investment trust savings plan statement of account

Date and transaction	*Share price (p)*	*No. of shares*	*Account change (£)*
24/11: Balance		0	0.00
15/12: Payment			50.00
21/12: Purchase	116.000	41	47.56–
21/12: Charge			1.15–
21/12: Stamp duty			0.24–
16/01: Payment			50.00
18/01: Purchase	120.000	41	49.20–
18/01: Charge			1.15–
18/01: Stamp duty			0.25–
14/02: Payment			50.00
22/02: Purchase	138.000	35	48.30–
22/02: Charge			1.15–
22/02: Stamp duty			0.24–
16/03: Payment			50.00
22/03: Purchase	144.000	34	48.96–
22/03: Charge			1.15–
22/03: Stamp duty			0.24–
05/04: Dividend			0.88
05/04: Balance		151	1.29

Source: Fleming Investment Trust Management Limited.

You will be kept informed of your share purchases with regular statements giving details of the number of shares bought, and the cost (see Exhibit 11.2). Normally at the end of each year you will be sent a single share certificate representing your holding accumulated throughout the year.

The schemes are very flexible because you can elect to make an occasional lump sum investment of £250 or more. You can also choose to have your dividends re-invested in the scheme or stop making payments into the scheme at any time without penalty. When it comes to selling your shares, most schemes offer special facilities to savers allowing them to take advantage of the same very cheap commission arrangements available when they bought the shares. It is worth checking for this because if the facility is not offered you will have to find a stockbroker to sell the shares on your behalf, which will be much more expensive. In these circumstances, in order to keep dealing costs to a reasonable percentage of your proceeds you should have at least £3000 worth of shares to sell of any one trust at any one time.

TAXATION

As far as tax is concerned, the cost of shares purchased, as detailed on your statement, will form the base cost of the shares for capital gains tax purposes. Dividends are paid or re-invested net of basic-rate tax and, as with unit trust schemes, you will receive a tax voucher showing the tax credit at the standard income tax rate. Tax can therefore be reclaimed by non-taxpayers and higher-rate taxpayers will be liable to a further tax payment in the normal way.

CHOOSING AN INVESTMENT TRUST

When choosing an investment trust you need to go through essentially the same steps as you would when choosing a unit trust (see Chapter Ten). Investment trust savings schemes should be treated as long-term savings plans and, as such, it is important to make sure that it is a suitable and appropriate investment for your particular circumstances.

Again you need to pick a trust that suits your objectives, and the categories of investment trusts are similar in many ways to those used by unit trusts. For instance, there are trusts which aim for capital growth through an international portfolio of shares and those that specialise in a particular geographical area. However, the emphasis in some of the categories is different – for example, there is a category for income growth as well as capital growth. Also, unlike unit trusts, investment trusts can invest directly in property and in securities which are not listed on a stock exchange. Some of the main categories are as follows: capital growth (e.g. general, international, North

America, Far East, Japan, commodities and energy); income growth; smaller companies; special features; and split capital.

RISK

As with unit trusts, the underlying investments determine the level of risk attaching to an investment trust and, as a guide, the categories you can expect to be less risky are the UK capital and income growth, UK income growth and those with a balanced international spread of equities. With investment trusts, however, there are two other important factors to consider when assessing risk – discount and gearing.

We have already looked at some of the effects of the share price discount to net asset value but, in simple terms, if you can pay for anything at below the going rate (i.e. at a discount) then you are getting a bargain. Many investment trust shares can be bought at a discount but, as a result of increasing demand, their share value can increase even if the underlying net asset value remains unchanged. In some instances this demand may even be strong enough to put the share price at a premium and so you will be paying more for the shares than the underlying assets are worth. These shares may still turn out to be an excellent investment, but there is still the risk that the share price could fall to a discount without any change in the asset value.

As briefly discussed earlier, unlike unit trusts, investment trusts are allowed to borrow money like any other company. They borrow the money in order to buy more investments and this ability to add gearing, as it is known, gives trusts that use it an added risk element. In a rising market, the shares of investment trusts with gearing go up by more than the value of their underlying investments, but the reverse is true in a falling market when the share price will fall further. In other words, shares of investment trusts with gearing tend to be more volatile than those without, and the more highly geared the trust, the more volatile the share price is likely to be.

MANAGEMENT GROUPS

There are now quite a number of investment trust companies offering regular savings schemes, but not all of them allow you to invest in their complete range of trusts. Therefore, in practice, the diversity of funds available to the regular investor is not quite as wide as with unit trusts. A listing of savings plans and the controlling management groups is set out in Exhibit 11.3.

Probably the best place to obtain performance statistics is from the Association of Investment Trust Companies (AITC). They produce a monthly information service

Exhibit 11.3 Investment trust savings plans (monthly minimum £25 or less)

Management group	*Monthly minimum*	*Lump sum minimum*
Alliance and Second Alliance Trust	£25	£250
Baring Private Investment Management	£25	£250
Fleming Investment Trust Management	£25	£250
Foreign and Colonial Management	£25	£250
Gartmore Investment and Scotland	£20	£250
Glasgow Investment Managers	£20	£200
Globe Management	£25	£250
GT Management	£25	£500
Guinness Mahon Fund Managers	£25	£250
Ivory and Sime	£20	£2000
John Govett and Company	£25	£250
Kleinwort Benson Investment Mngmt.	£25	£250
MIM	£20	£250
Martin Currie Investment Management	£20	£200
Scottish Investment Trust	£25	£250
Stewart Ivory and Company	£25	£250
Throgmorton Investment Management	£25	£250
Touche, Remnant and Company	£25	£250

Note: This table is intended only as an abbreviated guide to investment trust savings plans. Full details of individual schemes should be obtained before entering into any transactions.
Source: *Monthly Information Service, 28th February, 1990*: Association of Investment Trust Companies.

setting out share prices, net asset values, geographical spreads, discounts and gearing. There is a tick against those trusts which offer regular savings plans. The AITC should certainly be able to supply sufficient information to enable you to reach a well-informed decision. As with unit trusts, however, all you have to go on is past performance which, of course, is no guarantee of future results. But, again, choose a management group with a consistently good long-term record.

Having decided what plan you are going to invest in, fill out the form and send it off with a cheque for the first payment. Often you will have the choice of either having your dividends paid to you, or re-invested in the plan. It is probably best to re-invest the dividends until you have built up a sizeable sum. On retirement, for example, you can then change to having dividends paid out to you, at which point they will be a welcome source of extra income.

SUMMARY

Advantages

1. An excellent way of saving over the long term, with the value of your savings likely to keep pace with inflation.
2. Your regular contributions benefit from pound cost averaging.
3. The costs of investing in investment trust savings schemes are generally lower than for unit trust schemes.
4. The plans are flexible and you can stop your payments at any time without penalty.
5. A way of acquiring a broad range of professionally managed investments through a single shareholding.
6. In a rising market, investment trust share prices can rise at a faster rate than net asset values. This is where the discount can work in the investor's favour.
7. If an investment trust is standing at a discount, an investor will earn income on more assets than he or she actually pays for.

8. If demand for the shares increases for any reason, the share price can rise even though the trust's net asset value may be unchanged.
9. Closed-end fund status means that investment trust managers can take a longer-term investment view without worrying about investor redemptions or short-term performance.
10. In extreme conditions, it is easier to sell your investment trust holding than it is to sell a unit trust holding.

Disadvantages

1. Not suitable for short-term investment.
2. You must take care in the timing of your investment as most schemes only invest savers' funds once a month.
3. If the value of your shareholding is low, selling it through a stockbroker can be very expensive. You must therefore ensure that your scheme has a cheap selling facility.
4. The choice of funds available to invest in is less comprehensive than those available with unit trust savings schemes.
5. The discount can increase in a falling market and this can work against you.

As far as the regular saver is concerned, it is very difficult to choose between an investment trust and a unit trust savings scheme. Both types of scheme are very flexible, and in both cases your regular savings will benefit from pound cost averaging in asset-backed investments which are likely to hold their value over the long term. There have been surveys carried out by various publications comparing the performance, over a five-year period, of the average investment trust against the average UK general unit trust. They seem to suggest that investment trusts do perform marginally better. But at present, I believe that there is not enough data available to compare the savings schemes, nor to give any definite guidance, and therefore you should not read too much into these claims.

Because intermediaries earn a commission on unit trust purchases, it is sometimes easier to get clearly unbiased advice if you want to invest in investment trusts. Performance comparisons of investment trusts are published in a quarterly magazine called *Investment Trusts* (available on subscription from 120–126 Lavender Avenue, Mitcham, Surrey CR4 3HP) and the AITC issues a number of publications which you may be able to find at your local library. The Association's annual guide contains a section explaining how investment trusts work and gives comprehensive details of all the investment trusts and their track record. The Association's address is Park House, (6th floor), 16, Finsbury Circus, London EC2M 7JJ.

In conclusion, there is very little to choose between unit trust and investment trust savings schemes. Investment trusts do have some desirable qualities that unit trusts do not have, and for me this tips the scales in their favour. If, however, you find the concepts of discounts and gearing a little daunting, then you are probably best advised to stick to unit trusts.

12 Friendly Society Savings Plans

Surprisingly few people know about the savings plans offered by friendly societies. This is a shame, because the plans are investment gems which only very keen-eyed investors seem to take advantage of. You do not even have to be particularly well off to invest in these plans – currently, all you need is £9 per month or £100 per annum, although these amounts are due to rise to £13 and £150 respectively from autumn 1990.

The important advantage which the plans enjoy is complete freedom from income and capital gains taxes. Your money is invested in a tax-free fund and your return is paid to you tax free. This advantage means that your returns can be significantly better than with other savings schemes.

FRIENDLY SOCIETIES

The societies were originally set up to help poor families at times of sickness or death. In 1793 an Act of Parliament officially named them 'friendly societies' and granted them special privileges because of their charitable objectives. With the Poor Law Act of 1834 the societies became a major social movement providing monetary relief as well as social support for members. Their role was comparable to the welfare state of today. Because of their status, all profits were completely tax free. This benefit has continued up until the present day, although it has been severely restricted.

Life insurance companies pay tax on their investment profits before paying the proceeds to the policyholder, but with friendly societies the profits are tax free which means that there is more profit to distribute to policyholders. This is why the government has placed such rigid restrictions on investment.

Currently, friendly societies have about £4 billion under management, with the top 37 of the total of 500 or so societies accounting for 95 per cent of this sum.

HOW THE PLANS WORK

The tax-free savings plans offered by the friendly societies are restricted by law to one plan per adult. Anyone between the ages of 18 and 70 can invest, but if you already have a qualifying plan in existence with one society you cannot have another plan with a different society. A husband and wife can have a plan each.

The maximum investment is £9 per month over 10 years (to be increased to £13 per month if the 1990 Budget proposals are implemented). Your money is invested in a tax-exempt endowment policy, commonly unit-linked, with a specified maximum sum assured. With the unit-linked funds you can usually follow the prices of units in the *Financial Times*. Also, you are sent an annual statement showing the progress of your investment.

Data on the performance of friendly society unit-linked funds is included in *Money Management* (see the example in Exhibit 12.1). An up-to-date analysis of long-term performance will help you when choosing a society plan.

If you surrender your policy early be warned that, by law, the maximum encashment payment within the first 10 years is restricted to a return of your contributions. Friendly society plans are certainly a long-term investment and you must make sure you can easily afford the payments before you make a commitment.

At the end of the 10-year term you can continue paying premiums to increase your benefits, stop paying premiums and leave your money to grow tax free and cash it in any time thereafter, take a tax-free income from the policy, or

Exhibit 12.1 Friendly society fund data illustration

Friendly society	*Price*[1]	*Performance*[2]	
		6 months	*2 years*
Dominion Growth	70.9p	1020	945
Dominion Growth Exempt	98.0p	1045	967
Family Assurance A Bond[3]	544.6p	1042	1004
Family Assurance Cap Bond[3]	327.7p	1064	1095
Family Assurance Growth[3]	165.0p	1077	1005
Family Assurance Perf	105.5p	1049	1122
Hearts of Oak Tax Exempt	126.8p	1023	1176
HFS Managed 1 Tax Exempt	120.6p	1004	—
HFS Managed 3 Tax Exempt	124.1p	1016	—
Lancs & Yorks Bal Port[3]	135.8p	1044	1211
Lancs & Yorks Cap Secure[3]	216.6p	1024	1208
Lancs & Yorks Investor	101.9p	1266	1453
Lancs & Yorks Unitbuilder[3]	101.2p	1084	1409
Averages/Total funds		1058	1145

Note: Abbreviated data to 1st November, 1989, intended as an illustration only. Full and up-to-date data and information on individual schemes should be obtained before entering into any transactions.
[1]Offer price.
[2]£1000, offer to bid, net income re-invested.
[3]Regular premium life policy available.
Sources: FINSTAT and *Money Management*, December 1989.

withdraw all the proceeds free of tax. Once you cease to have a plan you may be eligible to start a new one.

RECENT DEVELOPMENTS

In addition to the increased investment limits put forward in the Budget, a January 1990 government Green Paper has proposed giving wider powers to friendly societies. If the proposals are implemented, the societies will be able to sell more products and a new regulatory framework will be introduced, including a compensation scheme and an ombudsman.

Any new legislation arising from the proposals in the Green Paper is unlikely to be in place before the summer of 1991 so we will have to wait and see what happens.

SUMMARY

Advantages

1. An excellent long-term investment with very important tax advantages. A must for all taxpayers.
2. Performance is enhanced by a tax-exempt investment environment.
3. All proceeds are free of tax.
4. An easily affordable plan.
5. Valuable life assurance is included without having to submit to a medical examination.
6. The plan is available to adults aged 18 to 70.

Disadvantages

1. Not suitable for short-term investment.
2. The maximum repayment values before maturity are restricted by law to a return of your premiums.
3. Contributions cannot be raised in line with inflation.
4. Friendly societies are not easy to find out about because they are rarely promoted by intermediaries or advertised in the press.

These friendly society plans offer very attractive tax-free investment opportunities that everyone should take advantage of. They are cheap and offer some life assurance along with an investment which, if unit-linked, could see the money you put in double in 10 years. You can leave your investment to grow tax free for many more years if you wish, which could provide a considerable extra sum for your retirement. Depending on when you take out your investment it could, among other things, help towards your children's education.

If you can afford to, you would be foolish not to take advantage of friendly society plans because you can never be sure if the tax advantages will always be available.

13 PEPs for the Regular Saver

Personal equity plans ('PEPs') were introduced by the Chancellor of the Exchequer in the 1986 Budget. The idea behind them is to encourage people to invest in shares by providing tax incentives. All income payments and gains on PEPs are free of both income and capital gains tax.

The maximum annual amount that can be paid into a PEP investing directly in shares is (following changes in the April 1990 Budget) £6000. However, many such plans insist on a sizeable lump-sum investment and therefore are beyond the scope of small, regular investors. I will therefore deal with the types of schemes that the regular saver might consider – namely unit and investment trust PEPs and managed portfolio PEPs.

UNIT AND INVESTMENT TRUST PEPS

The maximum you can pay into a plan investing exclusively in a unit or investment trust is £3000 per tax year (i.e. one-half of the overall annual maximum), or £250 per month. To qualify, a trust must have at least 50 per cent of its holdings in UK equities. As an alternative, you may invest up to £900 per annum in an investment or unit trust PEP that does not satisfy this 50 per cent rule (i.e. investing in foreign markets), but if you choose this option the remainder of your money will have to be invested directly into shares (not via a trust) up to the £6000 maximum. This means that you could invest a further £5100 per year into shares.

The plans are usually quite flexible, allowing you to top up your investment to the maximum amount throughout each tax year, which runs from 6th April to 5th April. You can also withdraw some or all of your investment at any time as far as is practically possible. It may take a couple of weeks before you actually receive your money.

Some PEPs let you invest as little as £25 per month, but the minimum contributions vary enormously between different plans. Once you have decided you can afford to invest, you select a trust from the choice available from the investment managers, and your monthly contributions are invested in that trust. Your contributions will therefore benefit from pound cost averaging, with all the advantages that were discussed in Chapter Ten.

Unit and investment trust PEPs, however, do have some weaknesses, notably that the investments are mostly concentrated in UK shares. For the small investor it makes sense to spread risk as much as possible around the stockmarkets of the world through a balanced international fund. The trouble is, if you do this, you limit your PEP investment in trusts to £900. Over the years, of course, it is possible to create a well-balanced investment portfolio through a PEP which can grow in a tax-free environment.

The tax concessions on a PEP mean that your investment dividends can build up free of income tax, which can be a big advantage for higher-rate taxpayers. The tax claimed back can then be re-invested in more units. Also, any capital gains you make will be exempt from capital gains tax. The impact of PEP tax concessions on a unit trust investment is shown in Exhibit 13.1.

Once you stop investing you have two choices: you can either cash in your investment with no tax liability, or you can leave it in its tax-free environment to accumulate for as long as you wish. PEPs can be used as a short- to medium-term investment, helping, for example, to pay for the children's education or, preferably, as a long-term investment (e.g. to provide some additional tax-free income or capital on retirement). If you treat a PEP as a long-term investment and hold it, say, for 10 years, you will make excellent use of the tax concessions which will

Exhibit 13.1 The impact of PEPs on a £1000 investment in the UK equity income median fund (figures to 1st October, 1989)

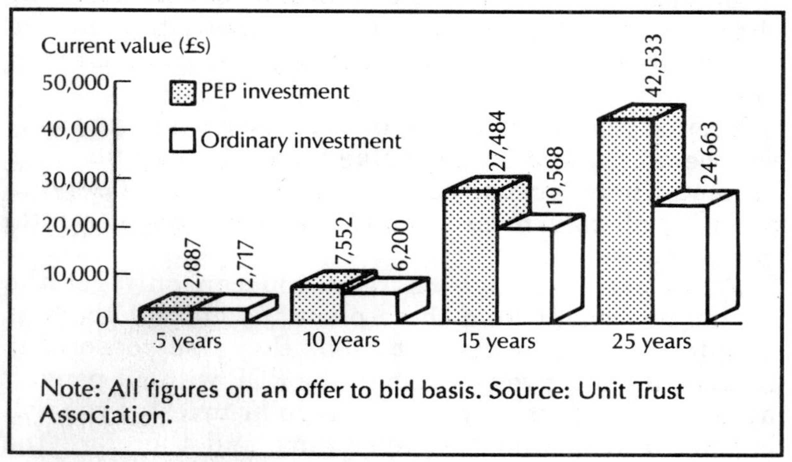

Note: All figures on an offer to bid basis. Source: Unit Trust Association.

help to increase the value of your investment at a faster rate.

There is one thing to watch out for – namely, that charges on these plans can be very high because of expensive set-up and administration expenses. I have come across some unit trust PEPs that have no extra charges for starting a plan (in other words, you only pay the normal unit trust charges), but these are the exception to the rule. Normally there is an initial and an annual plan charge. The lesson here is to read the small print and make sure you understand how much the charges are, as these can wipe out any tax advantages you might otherwise have expected.

MANAGED PORTFOLIO PEPS

This type of plan enables you to acquire shares in British companies, selected and managed for you by an investment management group. All investment decisions are taken on your behalf and there is very little paperwork to worry about. The maximum annual investment is

£6000, or £500 a month, but the minimum monthly investment is normally higher than for the unit and investment trust plans and could start from £50 per month. The charges on this type of plan are often higher than for the unit trust plans, so again make sure you know what they are.

Even if you are investing on a regular basis, you may still be able to top up your plan with a lump sum – the minimum here is usually around £200. As with other types of PEPs, all returns are free of both income and capital gains tax.

Because of the high charges, you can only get the maximum benefit from these plans if you treat them as long-term investments, although they are reasonably flexible, allowing you to cash in the PEP without penalty at any time. Again, if you are a regular investor you will benefit from pound cost averaging and therefore the timing of your investment is not as critical as it is for a lump-sum investor.

SUMMARY

Advantages

1. A plan with tax incentives to invest in equities, unit and investment trusts.
2. The income tax exemption on all dividends within a PEP benefits all taxpayers especially those paying higher-rate tax.
3. Those who normally use up their annual capital gains tax allowance each year benefit most from these plans because capital gains arising within the plan are also tax free.
4. PEPs are flexible and can be used as a medium-term investment, but ideally they should be treated as a long-term holding.
5. Regular statements keep you in touch with the returns on your money.
6. Regular savers benefit from pound cost averaging.

7. This is another plan that invests in asset-backed securities and, therefore, over the long term your investment has a good chance of producing a return better than the rate of inflation.
8. You can always get at your investment in an emergency.
9. Husbands and wives can invest up to a maximum of £12,000 in the 1990–91 tax year.
10. A marvellous opportunity to build up a portfolio of shares which in the long run could be extremely valuable. The portfolio of shares within a PEP is also much easier to manage, as the tax-free environment allows you to buy and sell shares on investment merits alone.
11. It is possible to take a regular tax-free income from your PEP.
12. PEPs can be used as a method of repaying a mortgage. Unit-linked and with-profits insurance funds used in endowment mortgages pay both capital gains and income tax and are therefore unlikely to perform as well as a PEP.
13. PEP mortgages are flexible because you can top up your contributions to the maximum allowed in order to help repay your mortgage quicker. This means that you are not restricted to repaying your loan at a set date.

Disadvantages

1. Charges can be very high and you must be aware of these when choosing your plan.
2. If you are not careful, charges may wipe out the tax advantages.
3. These plans are most suited to those who use up their capital gains tax exemption each year, and for higher-rate taxpayers.
4. The minimum investment may be too high for many regular savers to consider.
5. PEPs should not be considered as a short-term investment.

Anyone over the age of 18 who is ordinarily resident in the UK for tax purposes can take out a PEP. They are most suited to people who are higher-rate taxpayers, and those who normally exceed their capital gains tax exemption each year. These people will be able to make best use of the tax advantages that the plans have to offer.

But this does not mean that PEPs should be ignored by the less well off. On the contrary, anyone already investing in equities or considering doing so should jump at the chance to invest money on a tax-exempt basis. After all it is not often that the government gives us a tax break, and you never know how long these things will last. Once you have made adequate insurance and pension provision, a PEP should be one of the first investments for everyone to consider as a home for their long-term savings. Your investment will build up quicker than it would in an ordinary unit or investment trust savings scheme because of the tax-free environment, and over the years could rapidly grow into a very considerable sum. You can also use a PEP to progressively build up a substantial share portfolio which can be actively managed on investment criteria alone, without having to consider the tax implications of buying and selling shares. Above all, PEPs are flexible, allowing you to withdraw your money at any time (e.g. for emergencies) and they can also provide tax-free income.

PEPs are a relatively new product to the investment scene, and because of this the plans from different managers vary considerably. Some are more flexible than others, and the associated facilities offered may also vary. For this reason the charges differ a lot between management groups. You must take time to pick a plan to suit your needs and be sure you know what the charges are.

14 Pensions – The Fruits of Your Labour

Oh no – not a chapter about pensions! Many people have negative and preconceived ideas on pensions, and it is only when it is too late that they realise they have missed the opportunity of investing in one of the best and most tax-efficient forms of saving available. Yet again, we are returning to the subject of attitude. Retirement can seem such a long way off that we tend to think that planning for it can wait until much later. But pensions do not only concern older people. So how do you go about securing a good pension? Put simply, the more money you save the bigger your pension, and therefore the earlier you start saving the better.

The basic idea behind pensions is actually very straightforward – it is a means of giving up income now, in return for having an income in retirement. To compensate for locking up your investment for a long time the government grants tax relief on your contributions at your highest marginal rate. Not only that, but your investment has the advantage of growing in a tax-exempt environment. These two features make pensions one of the most tax-efficient ways of saving.

Unfortunately, many working people do not think about pensions until it is too late. The later you leave it, the more difficult it is to build up that lump sum. In fact retirement requires a lot of planning if you are going to enjoy life after work. Many people spend more time and effort planning their holiday each year than planning their retirement. But we should think of retirement as one very long holiday, not just 15 days, but 15, 20 or 25 years. It is something to be enjoyed and this means, among other things, being able to afford the things we want. The best holidays take planning and cost money, and the same applies to retirement.

Many retired people complain of not having enough to live on, which is very sad indeed. I cannot think of anything worse than working hard all your life only to end up at retirement having to scrape a meagre living. What is the point of the years of working if you have nothing to look forward to at the end of it? So, even when we are young and just starting out in a career, it is worth remembering that retirement can only be as good as the plans we make for it. If you think pensions are a luxury, consider what luxuries you might have to give up when you are living on one. After a lifetime of work, retirement should be a time to relax and enjoy life, just like a holiday.

Quite often the self-employed raise further objections about contributing to a pension. Some argue that they will be better off investing everything they have into their business, and when they want to retire they will simply sell the business and live on the proceeds. This is fine in theory, but who knows what the business will be worth in the future – in say 10 or 20 years time. It is not possible to know if it will still be going, let alone if it will still be prosperous. Even if it is successful it does not necessarily mean that the owner will get a good price for it and, in any case, he or she might want to pass it on to their children. If the self-employed looked at the subject of pensions in a more positive light they would see it as a means of taking some of the profit from their business, effectively tax free, and putting it to work in a tax-exempt fund which they should regard as an offshoot of their business. This will provide some money for them in their retirement, come what may.

The real sceptics amongst you will be saying 'What about the state pension – won't this be adequate to live on?' Well the fact is that it will not, as I am sure that those who have to exist on it will tell you in no uncertain terms.

THE BASIC STATE RETIREMENT PENSION

For 1990–91, the basic state pension is £46.90 per week for a single person or £75.10 per week for a married couple. But you are not entitled to this pension by divine right – you actually have to pay for it. To receive the full, 100 per cent pension you must have paid enough national insurance contributions. As a guide you should get the full pension if you have paid contributions for about 90 per cent of your working life. What is more, you can only start to claim this pension if you have retired and you are a man aged 65 or over, or a woman aged 60 or over.

Your working life is counted from the start of the tax year in which you reach 16 to the end of the tax year in which women reach 59 or men reach 64. Students are exempt, and if you have been sick or unemployed for any of the period you will be credited with the relevant contributions for that period. It is therefore important to realise that you have to keep up your national insurance contributions throughout your working life if you're to qualify for the full state pension. If you are going to live abroad for any length of time you must check with your Social Security Office to ensure you keep your full pension entitlement. There are two useful leaflets if you need more details – FB6 and NP32 – both issued by the Department of Social Security (the DSS).

If you are self-employed this basic pension is all you will be entitled to from the state, and if you have not made a substantial provision for retirement you will suffer a dramatic drop in income when you stop work. Even if you have paid for your house, there are still the other living expenses to consider, and you will find that these do not diminish to the same extent as your income. What happens if you need to run a car? Even paying for a colour TV licence will cost a week's pension for a married couple! Also, if you become frail and unable to cope on your own, will you be able to afford to pay someone to look after you? Certainly not on the basic state pension alone. It is true to say that the state has a duty to provide a basic income for retired people, but it is not obliged to maintain our standard of living at the same level as when we were working. It does, however, review the basic state pension once a year and, when necessary, increases it enough to maintain its value.

If you are employed, apart from the basic state pension you may also be entitled to an additional pension from the State Earnings-Related Pension Scheme, or SERPS. This additional sum may improve your lot, but you will still be faced with an unacceptable drop in income when you stop work.

SERPS

This scheme is sometimes referred to as the additional state pension and is the earnings-related part of your retirement pension. It is for employed people who have not contracted-out of the scheme, and depends on earnings since April 1978 on which Class 1 national insurance contributions have been paid.

The SERPS pension is only payable from state retirement age (65 for men and 60 for women) and in the 1990–91 tax year the lower earnings limit is £46 weekly, and the higher limit is £350 weekly. The difference between your earnings and the lower limit is called 'band earnings'. If you earn more than £350 weekly, then your band earnings are subject to the maximum. It's these band earnings for each year you work that are used to calculate your additional state pension. To offset inflation, they are increased in line with average earnings each year until the year in which you reach retirement age. A qualifying level for basic pension is then calculated and subtracted from your revalued earnings in each year to give a surplus figure. Each year's surplus figure, up to a maximum of 20 years, is added up and divided by 80 and it is this figure which becomes your additional annual pension. In simple language, SERPS will provide a pension of one-quarter of revalued average band earnings to everyone in the scheme for 20 years or more. The best 20 years of revalued band earnings are used, not necessarily the final 20 years.

Now here comes the twist. A while ago the government became very worried about the long-term cost of SERPS and under the Social Security Act of 1986 it reduced the benefits of all those retiring after March 2000. From then on the pension will be based on lifetime average earnings, and the benefits will decrease, over a period of 10 years, to one-fifth, not one-quarter, of revalued average earnings. So SERPS will be better value for employees retiring before 2000, while younger employees lose out.

Even with this additional state pension, employed people will still find that on retirement they face an unacceptable drop in income. For example, someone earning £15,000 per annum today can expect a drop in income of around 55 per cent when they retire and, obviously, the more you earn the bigger the percentage drop (see Exhibit 14.1). This could come as a rude awakening to anyone who has not made additional provision for their retirement. Let

Exhibit 14.1 The financial effect on employees of stopping work (in today's terms)

	Age[1]			
Earnings[2]	*Male*	*Female*	*Pension*[3]	*Income drop*
£10,000	30	25	£5446	46%
	40	35	£5531	45%
	50	45	£5778	42%
£15,000	30	25	£6457	57%
	40	35	£6726	55%
	50	45	£7010	53%
£20,000	30	25	£7106	64%
	40	35	£7442	63%
	50	45	£7798	61%
£25,000	30	25	£7106	72%
	40	35	£7442	70%
	50	45	£7798	69%

[1]Age in April 1990.
[2]Earnings assumed constant.
[3]Estimated additional pension plus basic state pension (married).
Source: Legal and General Group Plc.

us now look at ways we can go about making adequate pension provision.

COMPANY PENSION SCHEMES

These schemes are of two basic types – contributory or non-contributory. With a contributory scheme, as an employee you invest a percentage of your pensionable salary each month (commonly five per cent), with pensionable salary defined as annual salary less the lower earnings limit. With non-contributory schemes you do not pay anything. In both cases, your employer makes contributions into the scheme on your behalf. As long as the scheme meets certain requirements you will receive tax relief on your contributions and you will pay no tax on contributions made by your employer. Also, the pension fund itself is tax exempt.

This is, therefore, a very inexpensive way of providing for your retirement. To discover what sort of pension you will get on retirement you must find out what kind of scheme your employer operates. The most common type is the defined-benefit scheme.

DEFINED-BENEFIT SCHEMES

With defined-benefit schemes it is clear from the start what you can expect to receive by way of pension on retirement. It is usually a fraction of your salary for every completed year's service from the date you join the pension scheme. The fraction used by many schemes is one-sixtieth so, if you complete 40 years service, at retirement age your pension will be two-thirds final salary. Final salary is defined in different ways under different schemes. With some it is the average of the last three years' pensionable salary immediately before your retirement date. With others it may be just the salary in the last year before you retire (although this occasionally may include average overtime plus commission or bonuses during the final few years). You will need to check the details with your employer.

Although the benefits you receive on retirement are defined, they are subject to limits laid down by the Inland Revenue. For instance, provided you have completed at least 20 years service, you are limited to two-thirds of final salary, so if in the previous example an employee had completed 45 years service he could still only retire on two-thirds salary. However, the pensions benefits are based only on the first £64,800 of earnings, and therefore the maximum pension available is £43,200. Lower limits apply for shorter periods of service. This begs the question of whether you can take retirement before the normal state pensionable age. The answer to this is normally yes, provided you are aged over 60 for men or 55 for women, and have completed at least 10 years company service. You may be able to retire even earlier, but although your pension will be calculated as described, it will be reduced to take into account the expected longer period for which it will be paid.

You do, in fact, have a choice of how you wish to take your retirement benefits. You can either take the benefits as described above, or a part of your pension may be exchanged for a tax-free lump sum of up to 1.5 times final salary. The overall tax-free lump sum limit is currently £97,200. If you have completed less than 20 years service, and a maximum pension has not been provided, you may take a lump sum of three-eightieths of final salary for each year of service, with a maximum of 40 years. It is important to realise that if you do take a cash sum your company pension will be reduced accordingly.

OTHER COMPANY SCHEME BENEFITS

Company pension schemes often provide other valuable benefits besides a retirement pension. These include life insurance and it is important that you know the particulars to enable you to work out what additional life insurance you may need. If you die before retirement a cash sum of up to four-times your basic salary will be paid to your beneficiaries. On top of this, if you are married then a widow's or widower's pension may be provided, and this might typically be 25 per cent of your basic salary. If you die before retirement leaving dependent children, some schemes may pay an income for their benefit until they reach a certain age. There are often death benefits after retirement in the form of a widow's or widower's pension, which can be anything up to two-thirds of your pension, payable up until your widow's/widower's death. You may also be entitled to some disability benefits expressed as a percentage of your salary should you be absent from work for a prolonged period because of illness or injury. Your membership of the pension scheme will be maintained throughout the period of absence so that you will still be covered for death benefits.

Although the defined-benefit company schemes are the most common, it is worth mentioning another type of employers' scheme – the money purchase schemes on a defined-contribution basis. With this arrangement, both employee and employer pay a percentage of the employee's pay into the scheme, with the sum being specifically earmarked for that employee. The money is invested in a tax-exempt fund and on retirement the proceeds are used to buy a pension. How much the pension will be will depend on the performance of the fund, but the contributions are subject to maximum earnings limits as in defined-benefit schemes. The employee can obtain regular statements of the fund value and an estimate of the eventual benefits. He or she can also contribute up to 15 per cent of their salary into the scheme in order to increase overall benefits, subject to the maximum limits.

WHAT HAPPENS IF YOU CHANGE JOBS

Under a defined-benefit scheme you can suffer a substantial reduction in the value of your final pension if you leave your employer's scheme. The younger you are when you leave the scheme the greater the potential loss in benefits. This is because leavers' benefits do not increase as rapidly as the benefits of those who stay. When you remain with a firm your pension will increase each year in line with your earnings. However, if you leave, your pension, at best, will increase in line with retail prices.

Clearly, when you are young you have the potential to earn substantial increases in salary over the years, far in excess of increases in prices. In practice, most schemes do not even increase the benefits of leavers in line with prices but may offer to increase benefits by five per cent each year or in line with the RPI, *whichever is the lowest*. With most defined schemes there will be what is known as a transfer value as long as you have been in the scheme for at least two years. This monetary equivalent may then be transferred into your new employer's scheme. If you leave a company scheme within two years, you will probably be entitled to a refund of your contributions which would then be taxed at a special rate.

Under money purchase schemes your transfer value will be the value of the contributions you and your employer have made during your period of service, along with any increase in the value of your investment over that period. This type of company scheme is likely to give you a better transfer value than a typical final salary scheme.

We have seen how just changing jobs can reduce your company scheme pension benefits. Although this can be quite a serious problem if you have been a member of a number of defined-benefit schemes, you can do something about it by making additional voluntary contributions to enhance the value of your pension.

ADDITIONAL VOLUNTARY CONTRIBUTIONS

All employers' defined-benefit schemes allow members to make additional voluntary contributions ('AVCs') over and above their normal contributions. These are called in-scheme AVCs. These AVCs are subject to two major Inland Revenue limitations:

1. The employee cannot contribute more than 15 per cent of earnings in AVCs and pension plan combined; and

2. The total benefits provided by the AVCs and pension scheme together must not exceed the benefit limits set out by the Inland Revenue.

If the employee's AVCs perform particularly well and produce, with the main company scheme, a combined pension in excess of the two-thirds limit, the surplus is refunded to the employee in cash, less a tax deduction. AVCs qualify for tax relief in the same way as contributions to an ordinary scheme, but it is highly unlikely that your employer will contribute anything towards your AVCs. The money you save is invested in a tax-exempt fund as before, but you can choose how much you pay and when, subject to limits set by your employer and the Inland Revenue.

You do not actually have to make in-scheme AVCs. You can make them outside your pension scheme to a plan of your choice. These are usually available from life assurance companies, banks and building societies, and are called free-standing AVCs. You can use free-standing AVCs to contract-out of SERPS if the AVCs meet the requirements of an appropriate personal pension plan, but all new AVCs taken out, whether in-scheme or free-standing, cannot be used to increase the tax-free lump sum available on retirement. They may only be used to enhance pension benefits and provide life assurance cover.

As you can see AVCs can be a very valuable and tax-efficient way of enhancing your pension, especially when you can afford to save more from higher earnings. Those who benefit most are the higher-rate taxpayer and people who are in the years immediately approaching retirement. Younger people should bear in mind that money saved via AVCs can never be withdrawn prior to retirement and therefore they do not have the flexibility that you may need, especially if you have a lot of financial commitments.

PERSONAL PENSION PLANS

Nowadays you do not have to participate in your employer's pension scheme but, instead, can opt to take out your own personal pension plan. These plans can also be used to contract-out of SERPS (I shall cover this in more detail later) or by the self-employed to provide a fund for their retirement.

You can usually start to contribute to a plan at the age of 18, and it works like most other regular savings schemes, plus enjoying considerable tax advantages. In return for these generous tax concessions your money is tied up until you retire and you are also restricted as to how much you can contribute (starting at 17.5 per cent of your earnings, but this percentage rises once you are over 35 – see Exhibit 14.2). The restriction on contributions is also subject to a maximum earnings limit of £64,800. Personal pension plans are offered by investment organisations such as life assurance companies and unit trusts, and deposit organisations like banks and building societies.

HOW PERSONAL PENSION PLANS WORK

You agree to make regular monthly or yearly contributions (although lump-sum payments are permitted), and these are invested in a tax-exempt fund. This pool of money grows into a sizeable fund which is used to buy your pension when you retire. There is a choice of taking either a full pension or a tax-free cash sum and a reduced pension. The cash sum can be up to one-quarter of your pension fund, subject to a maximum limit per arrangement.

Exhibit 14.2 Personal pension plan earnings contribution limits

Age	*Percentage*
35 or less	17.5
36–45	20.0
46–50	25.0
51–55	30.0
56–60	35.0
61–75	40.0

Many modern policies are constructed as a cluster of a lot of separate arrangements or policies, and this can be used to very good effect because it lets you phase in your retirement over a period of time, and also take advantage of the maximum tax-free cash limit for each arrangement. The beauty about the modern personal pension plan is that you do not have to take your benefits at the retirement age you originally chose. Benefits can be taken at any age between 50 and 75. When you do decide to take your benefits, the cash fund is used to buy an annuity which will pay you an income for life. The return on annuities varies significantly from time to time, and between insurance companies, and for this reason many companies offer an open market option, meaning that they will let you shop around to secure the best pension. The most common type of annuity is a level annuity providing a very high income to start with, which remains level throughout. This may seem very attractive, but do not forget that inflation can erode the buying power of the income at an alarming rate. Alternatively, increasing annuities are available on which the income increases at regular intervals. A joint annuity is another possibility: this pays out until the person who bought it and someone else, usually a wife or husband, die.

PAYMENT OF CONTRIBUTIONS

It is best to make contributions on a regular basis, although it is possible to top up with lump sums. Most people prefer to invest monthly and the minimum contributions vary a lot between different companies. Some will allow you to invest as little as £10 monthly or £100 a year, but the minimum is more likely to be £25 per month.

If you are an employee, you will only pay, direct to your pension provider, the premium you have elected for, less income tax at the current basic rate (in other words, you pay your contributions net of tax relief). The pension provider will credit the full amount of your contributions to the plan and reclaim tax relief at the basic rate from the Inland Revenue. This is similar to the MIRAS scheme with building societies. Higher-rate taxpayers are able to claim the extra tax relief via their tax return. So, for argument's sake, let us assume that the basic rate of tax is 25 per cent. For every monthly contribution of £40, you need only pay £30 as the remaining £10 will be claimed by your pension provider from the tax man. If, however, you are self-employed, you will pay the full contribution to your plan and claim tax relief on the entire amount through your tax assessments.

There is one very important point to bear in mind concerning contributions. As I have said, you are allowed tax relief on a minimum of 17.5 per cent of your net relevant earnings in each tax year. (For employees, net relevant earnings can be defined as total non-pensionable earnings. For the self-employed, deductions can be made for expenses, stock relief or capital allowances, and losses normally allowed for taxation purposes.) But if you do not pay the maximum premium allowed in any year you can take up any unused relief from the last six years. Not many of us can afford to do this, but if you can it is well worth it. If you receive a large redundancy cheque, for example, you may decide to use some of the money in this way.

As with any other regular investment it is important that a pension plan is flexible enough to allow you to vary your contributions. You must take into account the effect inflation can have on contributions over such a long period of time. For this reason many companies offer the facility to automatically increase contributions in line with the Retail Price Index or, alternatively, by a fixed percentage each year. It is therefore important to pick a premium you can easily afford and increase it each year in line with inflation.

Although your contributions accumulate to provide a retirement income, this is not the only benefit that a personal pension plan can offer. It can be used to give security for your family should you die before retirement, in which case the full value of your pension fund would be used to provide benefits to your spouse or next of kin. On top of this, many plans allow you to arrange additional life assurance. Full tax relief is available on any contribution relating to this additional death benefit, although contributions are limited to five per cent of your net relevant earnings. Think carefully before you take up this option because the cost of the life assurance might be taking up a valuable proportion of your net relevant earnings, which could then no longer be used to provide a pension. For those who can afford to contribute the maximum to get the best possible pension, it is probably better to arrange extra life assurance separately.

Waiver of premium

There is one more feature that many of the more sophisticated personal pension plans offer, called waiver of premium. This is a way of insuring against not being able to work through illness or accident. After an initial period of incapacity, normally six months, you can cease making contributions but your benefits are kept up as if you had continued paying. This option involves the payment of a small additional charge and is a useful facility.

Once you have decided to invest in a personal pension plan you have to decide which kind. There are basically three types: unit-linked; with-profits; and deposit schemes.

UNIT-LINKED PLANS

Under a unit-linked scheme, you can choose from a variety of funds through which your money will be invested. Each fund is divided into units which have a bid and offer price in the same way as in unit-linked life assurance. The choice of funds is also similar (i.e. UK equity, managed, property, overseas equity, gilts and fixed interest).

After a deduction for commission and expenses your contribution is invested in one or more of the funds. The amount paid on retirement depends on how well the funds have performed. Over the long term, asset-backed investment performance is usually very good, but in the short term prices can go down as well as up and therefore there can be no guarantees of the amount paid on retirement. This can be a disadvantage because you may find that the value of your fund could drop in a bad year just before you retire. Unit-linked plans get around this by having a deposit fund which invests in bank and building society deposits. This offers a high degree of security over the short term and a steady, if unspectacular, return. You are sometimes allowed one free switch between funds each year, but thereafter there is a charge.

When choosing a unit-linked pension plan you must examine the charges carefully, especially when investing very small sums. Your pension could be severely affected by heavy charges. The difference between the bid and offer price of units is normally around 7 per cent but the annual management charges can vary widely, from 0.75–2.0 per cent of the fund value. When choosing a pension provider you must look at the charges very carefully.

Investment returns of pension providers also vary a great deal. Try to pick a company that has an above-average long-term record, using information from publications such as *Planned Savings* and *Money Management*. Past record is all you have to go on, and unfortunately it is no guarantee of future performance.

To sum up, unit-linked plans are a very good choice for those with at least 15 years to go before retirement because their long-term performance is likely to beat inflation. As you approach retirement you can always switch into a secure fixed-interest or deposit fund to consolidate the gains you have made over the years.

WITH-PROFITS PLANS

These are normally offered by life insurance companies. The pension at retirement is secured from a basic guaranteed sum, plus bonuses which will be added each year and will depend on the investment profits of the pension provider. Once added, these annual bonuses cannot be taken away, but future bonuses cannot be guaranteed. On retirement, an extra bonus may also be payable. With this type of plan you know from the start the guaranteed sum you will have available to provide for benefits at retirement. This plan is therefore much more suited to those who are about 10 years or so away from retirement and who would feel uneasy about investing in the more volatile unit-linked funds.

Some innovative pension providers have come up with plans that offer a unit-linked, with-profits fund. This enables a with-profits type plan to be part of a unit-linked structure, allowing unrestricted switching from one of the other funds to a with-profits fund, and vice versa. This provides more choice in your investment decisions and more security during the period leading up to retirement.

DEPOSIT SCHEMES

These schemes are offered by banks and building societies. They are usually very straightforward, without the added features of life insurance or waiver of premium, and therefore without the expense. Generally, no deduction is made from your savings to pay costs and commissions so all the money can be invested in your account. You earn interest free of income tax, which is credited to your account, thus adding to your pension benefits. The interest rates you receive will be higher than on other comparable accounts because they are tax free. If you die before retirement, all the money in your account will be used to provide benefits for your spouse or dependents.

This type of account is only attractive as a short-term investment because over the long term the rates of return are likely to be disappointing compared to market investments. Over the short term, however, deposit scheme returns are more certain and the charges are often minimal. The plans are ideal for periods within five years of retirement, using free-standing AVCs to top up your retirement benefits.

PERSONAL VERSUS COMPANY SCHEMES

If your employer offers a company pension scheme you have quite an array of pension provision choices. You can opt for the company scheme or make your own separate pension arrangements – but how do you decide what to do and what do you need to consider to arrive at the right decision?

For most people it will probably be better to join or stay in the company scheme, especially if it is a defined-benefit scheme. There are several reasons why this is so:

1. With defined-benefit schemes you know exactly the percentage of final salary with which you will retire.
2. With the better schemes, the pension benefits will increase during the contribution period, although rarely at the rate of inflation.
3. There will also be other benefits which would cost you more under a personal pension plan, such as death in service benefit.
4. Your employer will be making contributions and in the final salary schemes the company will undertake to make the necessary contribution to ensure that you receive the defined benefits.
5. The expenses of the schemes are normally borne by the employer.

If you choose a personal pension it is highly unlikely that your employer will contribute to it, so you would have to pay for any additional benefits independently.

Company schemes favour those who do not expect to change their employment and provide an even better deal for those who expect their future pay increases to be above average. If you require a high level of extra benefits for your family, joining a good company scheme would be very attractive and more cost-effective than securing the same benefits under a personal plan.

The only real problem with defined-benefit schemes is that changing jobs can have a detrimental effect on your pension benefits. But, as we have seen, this can be remedied by the use of AVCs. In short, a company scheme will provide the same benefits at less cost than a personal pension because you only pay a proportion of the cost while your employer makes up the difference.

THE ATTRACTIONS OF PERSONAL PLANS

Although a good company scheme will suit most people, personal pension plans have considerable advantages for others. If you are young and want to take an active interest in your investment then you should seriously consider a personal pension. You receive regular statements so you can see how your fund is progressing, and although investment performance varies widely, there is no limit on the benefits you can take from your plan. The only limitations are on your contributions. Therefore the younger you are and the more optimistic you are about investment performance, the more likely it is that a personal pension will suit you better.

If your plan performs particularly well, you may be able to take a bigger tax-free lump sum than if you had stayed in a company scheme. What makes personal pensions particularly attractive to the young is that they are fully portable, so you can change jobs as often as you like without affecting the value of your retirement fund.

The pension you receive with a personal plan will depend on two unknown factors: how well your investments perform up until retirement: and the level of annuity rates at that date. If you are prepared to accept the uncertainties then there is no problem. If they concern you then the performance projections of pension providers are unfortunately of very limited value because they have to be made on a standard basis using guidelines laid down by LAUTRO. You must always measure your pension as a proportion of final salary, and therefore you need to estimate what your salary will be at retirement by taking into account inflation. Your contributions must therefore keep pace with inflation and, if you are going to enjoy a really good pension, better it.

The flexibility of personal plans may also be attractive not just because of portability, but because you can add other benefits to the plan when you need them. For instance, you may be young and single and therefore there will be no need to provide benefits for dependents which a company plan might automatically include. Another possibility is using the tax-free sum on retirement to pay off a mortgage. This can be arranged with many lenders, although it should not be rushed into because it affects pension benefits. The other big advantage of personal pensions is that they are protected to an extent if your salary should fall in the period leading up to retirement. This can be quite a blow with a final salary scheme.

Now you have chosen what sort of pension you want, should you contract-out of SERPS?

CONTRACTING-OUT

It is now possible to contract-out of SERPS using your own personal pension. You still retain your rights to the basic state pension and any past SERPS entitlements, but you give up future entitlements to a SERPS pension. In return for this, you qualify for a rebate of some of your national insurance contributions – that is, the difference between the full rate of contributions both you and your employer make and the contracted-out rate. For the tax years 1988–89 to 1992–93 it is 2 per cent plus 3.8 per cent – i.e. 5.8 per cent. The government effectively contributes this rebate to your personal pension, but you will also get tax relief on your share of the rebate. The government is keen to encourage people to contract-out and so, as an added incentive, you may qualify for special bonuses payable until 5th April, 1993 (see Exhibit 14.3).

The exhibit assumes basic-rate tax of 25 per cent and band earnings of £2392–£18,200 per annum. These payments into your plan are known as protected rights contributions and the benefits from them are kept separate from other plan benefits, and may not be taken until state pension age. These benefits can only be taken in the form of a pension (not as a tax-free lump sum and reduced pension). The pension will increase by three per cent a year. You should remember that the pension from your protected rights depends on the value of the fund and the prevailing annuity rates when you retire and therefore, unlike SERPS, the value is not guaranteed.

Exhibit 14.3 Government pension plan contributions on contracting-out (£s)

Your earnings	National insurance rebate[1] Employee (2% of salary)	Employer (3.8% of salary)	Tax credit on rebate (0.67%)	Special bonus (2%)[1, 2]	Total contrib. (8.47%)
5,000	52.16	99.10	17.39	52.16	220.81
7,500	102.16	194.10	34.05	102.16	432.47
10,000	152.16	289.10	50.72	152.16	644.14
12,500	202.16	384.10	67.39	202.16	855.81
18,200+	316.16	600.70	105.39	316.16	1338.41

[1]Calculated on earnings that exceed £2392 per annum, but not on earnings that exceed £18,200.
[2]The special bonus is equivalent to 2% of your gross earnings between £2392 and £18,200 per annum. It is usually payable provided you have not voluntarily left your employer's contracted-out pension scheme after 5th April, 1988 having been a member for two years or more.
Note: All state benefits, national insurance contributions and rates of income tax are quoted for the tax year 1990–91.
Source: Rothschild Asset Management.

If your employer runs a defined-benefit pension scheme you may well find that it is contracted-out. In order to do this the company scheme has to meet certain conditions, the main one being that it undertakes to provide each member with the guaranteed minimum pension he or she would have received from SERPS. In effect then, the SERPS element is included in the total benefits provided by the company scheme. With a contracted-in scheme, an employee with maximum benefits could take two-thirds of salary, plus the benefits from SERPS and the basic state pension. With the contracted-out employers' scheme, the most the employee could achieve would be two-thirds of salary plus the basic state pension.

The decision to contract out of SERPS depends on three main factors:

1. Your age;
2. Whether you are entitled to the two per cent special bonus; and
3. Your expectations of future investment returns.

If you reach state retirement age in the year 2000, or just a few years later, you should stay in SERPS because you will almost certainly be better off. If you are younger, say 30–35 years away from retirement, the chances are that you could be better off contracting-out using a personal pension plan. If you fall somewhere between the two, and you are a cautious person, I would stay with SERPS because it is guaranteed, especially if you do not qualify for the two per cent incentive and you are pessimistic about investment returns.

Whatever you do, you need to consider all the pros and cons carefully before reaching a decision because getting it wrong could cost you a lot of money. Although the benefits from SERPS will be reducing after the year 2000, it does guarantee a level of benefits which are still attractive enough for many people in the scheme.

SUMMARY

Advantages

1. One of the best and most tax-efficient forms of saving available, offering full tax relief on contributions.
2. Your investments grow in a tax-free environment.
3. You can take a sizeable lump sum, tax free at retirement.
4. Your employer will contribute to an occupational scheme.
5. Income taken at retirement is taxed as earned income.
6. If you make your own pension arrangements you can take your benefits before the state pension retirement age.
7. Both occupational and personal pensions can provide valuable pre-retirement life insurance benefits.

8. The more you pay in, the more pension benefits you receive.

Disadvantages

1. Your benefits cannot be realised before retirement age or earlier death.
2. You cannot cash in your investment in times of hardship.
3. With personal pensions in particular, benefits depend on the value of your fund and the prevailing annuity rates at retirement. If investment performance is poor your pension could suffer a lot, particularly in the short term.
4. Not available to those without net relevant earnings.

Retirement is a time in your life when you should be able to sit back, relax and enjoy the fruits of your working life in comfort. It should be regarded as a very long holiday and as such requires careful planning and enough money so that you can afford to do the things you enjoy. With these aims in mind, this chapter has hopefully made clear that there is no possible way you can expect to live comfortably on the basic state pension alone, and yet this is all the self-employed will receive if they do not make further pension provision. Even those who retire with maximum additional state benefits will find that they will experience a totally unacceptable drop in income when they retire, and bear in mind that these benefits will be reduced after the year 2000.

The state will not look after you in the manner to which you have become accustomed whilst working, so everyone should do something about extra pension provision. It does not matter how little you save as long as you do something. Pension plans offer an excellent savings vehicle for retirement but unfortunately there are some people who are not allowed to contribute to these schemes because they have no net relevant earnings. The most unfortunate in our society, such as the unemployed, come in this category and cannot contribute to pension plans, even if they could afford to do so. Instead they somehow need to regularly put a few pennies aside into one of the other low-instalment methods of saving I have discussed in Part II, and they should at least ensure that their entitlement to the basic state pension is kept intact by getting in touch with the DSS.

There is no doubt that choosing the most suitable pension for your needs can become very involved and complex because there are so many facts to consider, and choices to make. You will probably want to discuss things with a financial adviser before you come to a decision, but once you have decided what to do, do not delay. Don't forget, the more you save, the longer you save, the better your pension. Time costs money.

PART III

HOW TO USE YOUR CHOICES

15 Putting Plans Into Practice

This book is all about saving and, in Part I, the challenge was set – to make yourself substantially better off. In Part II we discussed some of the tools you can choose from in order to meet the challenge and, in this final part, I shall attempt to explain how you can use those tools to finish the job. Learning when to use particular financial products is also important because some investments are wholly inappropriate at one stage in our lives but essential in other circumstances.

At the start of this book, I talked about building up a financial map of our affairs. Here, in Part III, I will try to help you to continue to find a route on the map even after it changes at different stages of life, presenting financial problems and obstacles that will have to be overcome if your goals are to be achieved. This will help you plan your savings to suit your situation and also, should you visit a financial consultant, you will be more able to ask the right questions and get the right products for your needs.

A CONCEPT OF FINANCIAL PLANNING

Not everyone needs the services of a financial consultant to plan their savings strategy, as long as they are asking themselves the right questions. Even then, however, a consultant may be useful as a source of quotes for comparing products and for fine tuning your investments.

A friend of mine told me this tongue-in-cheek definition of a financial consultant: 'Someone who looks at your watch and tells you what the time is.' In financial terms, the analogy of the watch might be your savings and investments or assets and liabilities. If your savings and investments become out of step with your goals, then your financial watch has stopped, and you will need to ask somebody for the correct time. You may, however, know what the time is and why your watch has stopped and it may be that all you need is a new battery – as long as you get the right one your problem is solved. On the other hand, everyone's financial watch is different and not many people know how to repair it if it goes wrong, and this is where the financial consultant comes into his own. A consultant should examine your financial situation, see the problem and solve it.

In this section my aim is to highlight the various goals you may wish to set yourself as you go through life. Having read the whole book it may well be that you feel confident enough to pick the right financial products to meet your needs.

ASKING THE RIGHT QUESTIONS

As we progress through life we all find that our circumstances change, either dramatically – for instance a change of job or getting married – or situations develop whereby we realise we have more or less to spend each month. At each change we need to ask ourselves certain questions so that we can plan our finances and get the best out of our money.

First of all, ask yourself what plans you have for both yourself and your family and try and split these into short- and long-term. This will tell you what you want to do with your money, and from this you can work out how much you can afford to spend and how much is left over to save. Short-term plans might include taking a holiday abroad each year, in which case you can set a financial goal of saving a certain amount each month so that you can afford to go. A long-term plan may be to retire at 60 and, again, it is a question of setting financial targets in order to achieve this goal.

Once you have worked out how much you can easily afford to save regularly, set aside at least some of the money to pay for long-term objectives and use the rest for your short- to medium-term plans. Once you know for how long you want to invest your money you can start to narrow down your choice of investments considerably. If there is a possibility of needing cash quickly, it is no use putting those savings into a 10-year endowment plan. If it is going to take just two or three years to save up for a new car, choose a suitable product from the banks, building societies or National Savings where your money is easily accessible.

This leads on to the question of how much risk one is prepared to take – the more long term your investments are, the riskier you can afford to be. The risk of equity-based investments, such as unit trust savings plans, may be acceptable because, potentially, they may perform much better in the long term than money in the building society. It is important not to forget, however, that in an emergency you may unexpectedly need to get at the money quickly and this may mean having to sell investments after a period of poor market performance. Some people are not prepared to take such risks and, therefore, their investment choices are very limited. If you are uneasy about equity-based investments you should stick to what you are comfortable with – an above-average return may not be worthwhile if it is acquired at the expense of your nervous system.

Investment choices can be narrowed down even further by an individual's tax position. For instance, a higher-rate taxpayer may find some of the tax-free investments offered by National Savings particularly attractive, and although the quoted rate of return may seem lower than that of a bank account, the net return may well be higher. There are many 'tax-free' investments discussed in this book, and whether you decide to choose one or not may well be determined by how much tax you pay.

Here is just a quick summary of the questions you should ask yourself:

1. What are your plans and what do you want to do with your money?
2. What targets will you set yourself?
3. How much can you easily afford to save on a regular basis, or how much do you need to save?
4. How long are you prepared to tie your money up. Do you need a short-term or long-term investment?
5. How much risk do you want to take?
6. How much tax do you pay?

Every time you review your finances, ask yourself these six questions to check that everything is going according to plan. Not having a plan means you run the risk of becoming financially lost and this dramatically reduces the chances of ever being better off. Try to review your finances at least once a year, or every time your circumstances change – for instance, when you get a bonus or a pay rise, or cash in some savings.

A LIFETIME OF CHANGE

Everybody goes through many changes in circumstances which can present considerable financial problems as we journey through life. Although people's aims, attitudes and priorities vary, in discussing 'How to use your choices' I think it would be helpful to follow through the various stages of a typical life. You may be able to recognise the particular point you have reached and check to see if you have thought about the financial implications I talk about here, and how decisions might affect your future plans. Hopefully, this exercise should help you to ask the right questions, keep your finances on course, and so plan for a wealthy future.

16 Your First Job

When you start your first full-time job you can look forward to a regular income at the end of each week or month. For most people this is money of their own that they have never had before, and it is treated as a bit of a novelty. Most youngsters have few, if any financial commitments and, once they have paid for their keep, the rest of their income is often regarded in the same way as pocket money which they used to spend as a child. In these circumstances, few people have much idea about how to handle their new found wealth – they are not taught it at school and are expected to find out as they go along. Here are a few pointers.

At this stage, the key to making the best use of your money is to budget for everything, even if you have few commitments. To start with, you may have only one or two items for which to budget (e.g. board and lodgings, clothes and leisure); these are just your immediate, short-term needs and objectives. Other young people may also have very fixed ideas as to what they want to do over the next few years. A priority may be to buy a car, take a year off and travel the world, or perhaps to buy a home of their own as soon as possible. These items fit into a longer-term plan, and also need budgeting for – and once you know what you want to do with your money you can start to save effectively.

SUITABLE SAVINGS VEHICLES

At such an early stage in their lives, most young people are fairly unsettled and find it difficult to predict or plan for what they will be doing in a year's time, let alone for the rest of their lives. For this reason they should start saving most of their available money in a savings vehicle that offers a reasonable rate of return, but also offers easy access – the ability, if necessary, to get at the cash quickly. As discussed in Part II, the banks, building societies and National Savings between them provide a whole range of products to fit the bill. You will be surprised how quickly your savings grow if you set some money aside on a regular basis.

It is also important to build a sizeable emergency fund in case of unemployment or other unforeseen difficulties and, even at this stage, to divert at least some of your resources into a longer-term savings plan. This can be used to build up a deposit for a house, for capital to start a business, or any number of things. As I have said many times throughout this book, investments which tend to do better over the longer term are asset-backed, and if you are the sort of person who can live with the added risk, this is the type of investment to seek out. Personally, I would tend to favour investment trust or unit trust savings plans at this stage, because they do not involve paying for unnecessary life insurance and do not impose early encashment penalties.

So in conclusion, even at this early time in your life, you should have both long- and short-term savings, both of which are flexible enough to cope with any rapid changes in your circumstances.

17 Newly Married and Starting a Family

Once a person has settled into a job and married, they usually find that they have a whole new series of responsibilities and financial commitments that can make previous financial plans obsolete.

In many cases, initially both partners are earning and hopefully by this time have enough money set aside to put down as a deposit on a home. With two sets of earnings it may be relatively easy to afford the interest payments, but if the couple plan to have a family they will need to be able to cope on just one salary.

Many people nowadays choose to buy a home via an endowment mortgage. An endowment policy is taken out to cover the mortgage so that at the end of the term there is a sum available to pay off the loan and, in some cases, if the policy has performed well, there may be an additional lump sum to look forward to. With many of the modern policies you can choose when you want to pay off your mortgage, even if you move and borrow more money. For married couples it is probably best to have a joint life policy so that the survivor of the husband or wife is able to repay the mortgage in the event of their partner's death. This is vitally important if your partner's income is needed to enable mortgage payments to be met. This leads on to questions you must ask yourself if you are planning to have a family. For instance:

1. How would your partner and children cope financially if you died tomorrow?

2. How would you cope if your partner died leaving you with young children to look after? Could you afford a full-time nanny?
3. Do you really want to take the risk of your family being forced to struggle to survive on state benefits only?

WIDOWS AND WIDOWERS

It is well known that, on average, women tend to live longer than men, and when this is added to the fact that men often marry women younger than themselves, the probability is that it will be the woman who will end up living her final years in solitude.

The number of widows in Britain runs into millions: their circumstances limit their earning power and, therefore, if they have not made provision for when their husband dies, all they have to look forward to is a very meagre existence on state benefits. I feel particularly sorry for young widows with children to bring up, for they usually suffer the most.

These are sobering thoughts that couples simply must discuss when they get married, and because the husband usually dies first, the wife must make sure that she is involved in making appropriate financial arrangements. If a wife works together with her husband on family financial matters it will make matters easier for her if she has to cope with the finances on her own. It is worth examining what doing nothing and relying on the state means in this context.

Widows' payment

This is a tax-free, one-off payment to widows aged less than 60 when their husband dies. The amount for 1990–91 is £1000, which assumes the widow's late husband had met the minimum national insurance contribution conditions. It might be enough to pay for a very modest funeral, but that is about all.

Widowed mothers' allowance

This is a taxable regular payment of benefit which, for 1990–91, is £46.90 plus £9.65 per child per week. It is only payable to widows with dependent children or to those expecting their late husband's baby and is a contributory benefit, which means that widows can only claim it if their late husband met the required national insurance contributions.

Widows' pension

In general terms, if a widow under age 60 stops receiving the widowed mothers' allowance because she no longer has a dependent child, she may be entitled to the widows' pension. It is not possible to receive both benefits at once. Again this is a taxable, contributory regular payment. The standard rate for 1990–91 is £46.90 per week. Widows are entitled to this benefit if they are 45 or over when their husband died (and they may also qualify if they are over 60 but under 65 and their husband had not retired at the time of his death).

Widowers

Men who are widowed after they have retired, and their family has grown up, are generally not too badly off financially as long as they have made reasonable provision. However, if men are widowed and have no choice but to stay at home and look after young children, the family will be forced to survive on the minimum levels of state benefits. There are no special allowances for widowers as there are for widows, so they can be considerably worse off.

To sum up, you will not get rich on state benefits if your partner dies. For a start the state is not obliged to maintain your living standards at the level to which you may have become accustomed and, in any case, you have to qualify for the benefits – not everybody does. Widowers left with a young family are particularly hard hit, and widows under 45 with no children are entitled to the widows' payment only. (For more details of these benefits see leaflets NI196 and NP45 from the Department of Social Security.)

A CHECKLIST FOR MARRIED COUPLES

Married couples should aim to arrange their financial affairs in such a way that they will be able to cope in the event of their partner's death – and that means both husband and wife. This is particularly important where children are involved. We have already seen how desperate the situation can be for those left to get by on state benefits alone. It is bad enough coping with grief, let alone poverty as well. So what can be done to solve these problems?

First, make a will. If you do not, the law provides for your assets to be passed on according to certain rules laid down by the state. These rules are varied and complex, depending on the value of the estate that you leave, and who is left behind. People assume that if they do not make a will then everything will pass to their spouse. In fact, it only needs one close relative to be alive for your wife or husband not to receive everything (although they will usually receive the largest share of the estate). If, for instance, the family home is worth more than your spouse's strict legal entitlement, it would have to be sold. The point is, it could leave your loved ones in serious financial difficulties and with serious practical problems. Also, you do not have to be particularly well off for this type of thing to happen.

The answer, therefore, is to make a will ensuring that your money and assets go where you want when you die, and not as the state specifies. You can choose the people who will administer your estate and arrange a financial plan to suit your family needs. Failing to make a will can increase the liability to inheritance tax and can make your estate more expensive to administer. It takes time and money to divide up an estate, and if you are not careful your dependents may be left without enough money for day-to-day living expenses. Frankly, therefore, it is irresponsible for a husband and wife not to make a will.

For couples buying a house, the next thing on our checklist is to make sure that the mortgage can be repaid in the event of either the husband or wife dying. Many people achieve this by having an endowment mortgage and using a joint life policy to provide the protection they need.

The third point at this stage is to check your pension arrangements, particularly the husband's. A lot of defined-benefit company schemes offer excellent value for money, and provide considerable family benefits in the event of a husband's death. The benefits on their own are not normally enough to provide adequate money for the beneficiaries, but they help considerably. If you do not have access to a good company scheme you must make your own arrangements. Again you can use your own personal pension plan to provide considerable death benefits.

Another important point is to make sure that both husband and wife has adequate life insurance cover. The younger you are when you take out life insurance the cheaper it will be, and the greater the level of benefits provided. Take out a good endowment policy at first so that initially you can take advantage of the protection element and then, when the family has grown up, you can both look forward to a nest egg when you retire. If you have children, you can top up with cheap term assurance to provide the added protection you need.

As you can see, therefore, when you get married the balance of your savings changes dramatically, moving from predominantly short term, when you are young, free and single, to long term, leaving just a small percentage of total savings for short-term use. This is why most people find it a financial struggle when they get married and start a family – there are often too many bills to pay and too many things to budget for, and not enough resources.

Some people may have further plans – for instance, parents sometimes want to provide their children with a lump sum when they come of age in order to give them a good start in life. Many life insurance companies offer suitable savings plans for this. Other parents may want their children to receive a private education. To do so, they should start planning for school fees as soon as the child is born, either by using with-profits endowment plans or a specially designed school fees plan.

PERMANENT HEALTH INSURANCE

Another thing well worth considering is permanent health insurance ('PHI'). In return for regular premium payments, if for any reason you cannot work because of sickness or accident you will receive a regular income which will go on for as long as the incapacity continues, or until you reach a particular pre-set age. Usually the payments start after a three- or six-month deferred period. Again, the younger you are when you start paying the premiums, the cheaper it will be.

PHI is rarely talked about and few people make any provision for incapacity preventing them from working. If you are unable to work for a long period then state benefits will not be enough to maintain your standard of living. It makes sense to provide for this eventuality because, based on established statistics, you are much more likely to be prevented from working for long periods because of illness or an accident than you are to die before reaching retirement age.

When you take out a policy you choose the level of income benefit, but there is a maximum limit of 75 per cent of your earnings at that time. When calculating income benefit, the insurance company will also take into account any state benefits you are receiving as a result of your incapacity. Many modern policies offer an indexation option which means that the level of income benefit under the plan is increased each year in line with inflation before and during the period for which it is paid. To pay for this, your contribution will increase slightly each year, but it will mean that your benefits, should you need to make a claim, will have maintained their real value. Most policies also allow you to top up your benefits for a small additional premium, and this is particularly useful if, for example, you have had a job promotion.

When you consider how important it is, as far as possible, to guarantee the level of your income, it makes a lot of sense to take out PHI, especially when you are young and healthy and the premiums are very low. In an ideal world these income protection plans would become an integral part of everyone's financial planning.

But if you feel your resources cannot stretch to PHI, you may instead consider taking out a very cheap hospital cash plan which will pay out a sum of money for each day you spend in hospital as a result of an accident. (Bear in mind, however, that nowadays it is very rare for people to spend more than two weeks in hospital.) These plans will often pay out a reduced sum while you are convalescing, up to a maximum time period equal to the number of days spent in hospital. Personal accident and sickness policies go a bit further – they will normally pay out for periods up to two years. These types of policies are no substitute for PHI, but they can provide valuable short-term benefits at very low cost.

Checklist summary

1. Have you made a will and, if so, does it need reviewing?
2. Would your mortgage be fully repaid in the event of your spouse's death?
3. What pension arrangements have you made?
4. Do you have adequate life insurance cover?
5. Do you have any other plans for which you need to provide?
6. Do you want to protect your standard of living in the event of sickness or accident?

WHAT IS ADEQUATE LIFE INSURANCE?

I have discussed at length in this book how life insurance policies can be used to build a substantial lump sum, but how much life assurance do we need to protect against the possibility of dying too soon? Few people have any idea how to calculate this, but it is really quite simple.

First of all, whether we actually need life insurance or not depends on individual circumstances. For a young person with no ties or responsibilities, life insurance on its own is wholly inappropriate and there would be better ways to invest the money. Once married, couples certainly need to consider protecting their dependents. It is important that both husband and wife plan their life insurance needs together.

What both partners need to do is to consider carefully how they would cope financially if their spouse died. This is especially important where there is a young family. To calculate what replacement income would be required, use the budgeting checklist in Chapter Four (Exhibit 4.1). It may be that if you are buying your home you have a mortgage protection policy or an endowment mortgage that will pay off the loan should one or other spouse die. This will reduce living expenses but it will not eliminate them (of course, if you are renting then there will be no change). In fact, most other costs will either stay the same or only reduce slightly – some may actually increase. From a wife's perspective, if you are a working mother you will probably need to employ a child minder each day until you finish work and these services are not cheap. Also, the chances are that general maintenance and repair costs are going to be much higher, and so an increased total will need to be entered in this column. You may also need better holidays and weekend breaks to help relieve the stress caused by grief.

From a husband's point of view, he is almost certainly going to have to employ someone to look after the children and keep the house in order, and he also will probably spend more on holidays and short breaks. Even when there are no children the inevitable bills still need to be paid.

Once you have worked out how much a year each partner would need to survive comfortably, the next step is to work out how big a lump sum investment is needed to produce that annual income. In asking the question, 'What annual rate of return can I reasonably expect to get on my money?' do not forget to take into account the effects of inflation, because the amount that you need to live on will have to increase each year to keep pace. A realistic return for an increasing income would be about five per cent per annum. Thus, to generate an income of £5000 initially, would require a lump-sum investment of £100,000 and this would be the life cover needed.

A simpler method of calculating life cover is to divide how long it will be before your youngest child is likely to become financially independent: this could be at 21, after university or college, or it could be earlier. If, for instance, it will be 12 years before your youngest starts earning their own way in life, multiply the income you need each year (say, £10,000) by 12; this will give you the amount of life insurance you will need (i.e. £120,000). This total does not take inflation into account which is why it is so important to review life insurance regularly. These figures may seem a lot but compare them to how much money you will take home throughout your working life (see Exhibit 17.1).

Many people say that they cannot afford to be fully insured, but if your family had a machine which earned hundreds of thousands of pounds throughout its lifetime (your spouse) wouldn't you think it a sensible idea to insure it for what it is worth? Bear in mind also that a

Exhibit 17.1 If you earn money, what are you worth to your family?

	Pre-age 65 total take home pay (£s), based on current annual take home pay of:			
Your age	*£4160*	*£5200*	*£7800*	*£10400*
20	187,200	234,000	351,000	468,000
25	166,400	208,000	312,000	416,000
30	145,600	182,000	273,000	364,000
35	124,800	156,000	234,000	312,000
40	104,000	130,000	195,000	260,000
45	83,200	104,000	156,000	208,000
50	62,400	78,000	117,000	156,000
55	41,600	52,000	78,000	104,000

family man under the age of 30 can probably insure himself fully for less than the cost of insuring the family car, which is a depreciating asset.

You can reduce your insurance costs if you have already made provision to have your mortgage repaid in the event of your spouse's death. You can cut it back further by making a list of your assets, such as death benefits from your pension and other life insurance policies and the value of your remaining investments.

ADMINISTRATIVE ARRANGEMENTS

Discovering how much life assurance you need is not quite enough on its own. When you take out a policy it is important to make sure the money will be paid to the right people at the right time. One way of achieving this is to have the policy held under the terms of a suitable trust. Take the example of a husband who has a policy which assures his life for his own benefit. On the husband's death the insurance company would pay whatever money was due to his family as soon as possible, but without using an appropriate trust the company must wait until the estate has been formally dealt with before it can pay the next of kin, and this process can take months. To avoid the delay, the husband should take out a policy written under the Married Woman's Property Act, 1882, which assures his life for the benefit of his wife and children. The proceeds in this case do not pass through the estate of the deceased, but go directly to the beneficiaries.

The other advantage is that the proceeds do not attract inheritance tax. A life assurance adviser will help you in writing a policy in trust – it is not as difficult as it sounds and is certainly worth doing.

To put things into perspective, you should only put aside for life insurance a proportion of your income that you can easily afford to commit. It is, after all, only one of many things to budget for. If you can afford to be fully insured then do go ahead. However, many of us have to make the best of what we have got and this usually means making some sort of compromise.

18 Pre-retirement

Pre-retirement is defined here as the period beginning when your children leave school and are able to look after themselves, up until the time you retire. As your children become more responsible for running their own lives, your own financial commitments will start to diminish and you will have more money to spend as you wish. It is during this stage of life that you will hopefully have a little more cash for luxuries, and it is also another appropriate point to take stock of your financial position.

If your earlier financial planning has been successful you should be in a position, before retirement, to pay off your mortgage, which will be a major saving. If you have term insurance policies providing extra cover for the children you should safely be able to let these lapse. Therefore, if everything has gone according to plan, you will have more to save as well as more to spend, and you should be looking to invest these savings wisely as retirement looms nearer.

PRE-RETIREMENT STRATEGY

The first point is to ensure you are making maximum use of your pension contribution limits. Don't forget that a pension is one of the most tax-efficient ways of preparing for retirement, and if you are in a company scheme consider taking out a free-standing AVC (additional voluntary contributions) to top up your benefits (see Chapter Fourteen). If you have a personal pension you may decide to become more cautious in your choice of investment funds, switching from higher-risk to lower-risk funds in the run-up to retirement in order to consolidate the growth your fund has achieved. You must try and avoid being forced to take your pension soon after a large fall in the stockmarket, and therefore the closer you get to retirement the less risky your investment strategy should become.

It is also worth considering putting some extra money aside using a with-profits endowment savings plan: this will provide a known extra lump sum on retirement. If you have been under-insured in the past, this is a good way of topping up your life insurance and saving at the same time. Also, the pre-retirement years could be a time when you are a higher-rate taxpayer, and therefore you should try and make maximum use of all the available 'tax-free' investments, particularly some of the National Savings products (see Chapter Eight).

'BUT WHAT IF ....'

It is all very easy isn't it? Naturally I have assumed in the preceding paragraphs that, from school-leaving age, you have planned your finances to perfection and that all you need to do now is a little bit of fine tuning so that you can retire with a lot of money and live happily ever after. But for a lot of people this scenario bears no resemblance whatsoever to reality: indeed, if it applied as far as you are concerned, you probably would not be reading this book.

A much more likely scenario is as follows: you are middle aged, 21 yet again next year, with children growing up and leaving home, and you have suddenly realised that, as each year passes, retirement is thundering towards you like an express train: if you do not do something about financial planning now, you are not going to be able to avoid a head-on disaster when retirement day finally hits you. Recognising that you may have some financial problems is a major first step and, if you have about 15 years or so to go before state retirement age, then there will be time in which to start putting things right – so there is no need to panic yet!

PENSIONS

First, if you are not a member of a company or personal pension scheme, then join a pension plan right away. The sooner you start the greater the retirement benefits will be and do not worry if, for now, you can only contribute the minimum amount. Any delay can make an enormous difference to the eventual benefits.

Many of the modern pension plans are very accommodating, allowing you, for example, to incorporate extra life cover into the plan if you wish. You are allowed, at any age, to contribute up to 17.5 per cent of your earnings into a pension, but this limit rises in stages from the age of 35, reaching 40 per cent at ages 61–75 (see Exhibit 14.2). This is a particularly useful concession for those who have taken out a pension plan rather late in the day: it means that if they are lucky enough to have a sizeable lump sum which they can do without until retirement, then it can be invested in the scheme. Full tax relief is available on the money and it will be able to build up in a tax-exempt environment.

If you belong to a company pension scheme and see yourself staying with the company until retirement, you should consider topping up your pension benefits by making additional voluntary contributions – perhaps via a free-standing AVC (see Chapter Fourteen). This is particularly important if you have not been in the scheme for very long. Additional contributions can make a significant difference to your benefits at retirement.

MORTGAGES

The next thing to consider is your home. Many of you will probably be buying your own house or flat and will have a mortgage. The object of the exercise is to pay off the mortgage before you retire, so that you will have more spending money each month and more to invest for the future. The fact is that unless you are extremely fortunate, you are likely to suffer a drop in income on retirement, and having to pay the same bills on a lower income is not a good idea. The earlier you are able to pay off the mortgage the better, so if you are in a position to consider this then do go ahead.

If, on the other hand, you rent your home and intend to continue doing so, your pension in retirement has to be able to cope with a regularly increasing rent bill. In these circumstances, it is even more important that you retire with very substantial funds, comfortable in the knowledge that you will be able to afford rent increases when they occur.

Up until now, I have been considering longer-term investment planning for those who have 10 years or more to retirement. But do not forget that shorter-term investments are also important – it is always a good idea to retire with a sizeable emergency fund because, human nature being what it is, we tend to live up to our income without leaving much room for manoeuvre. If you have used an endowment policy to pay off the mortgage, you may well find that you have an additional lump sum which can be used for this purpose. Perhaps more by luck than judgement, there are a few insurance policies in a drawer somewhere which are due to mature shortly. Do not rush out and spend the money at once, but consider carefully, as retirement rapidly approaches, how it could be used. Also, why not continue saving the money that used to be employed on funding the policies in another appropriate savings plan (e.g. a PEP, a friendly society, or a unit or investment trust plan).

If you have less than 10 years to go until retirement, then the options are severely restricted. If you enjoy good health, you may have to seriously consider postponing retirement and working a bit longer. However, steps taken now can still make you far better off than if you do nothing at all. Concentrate on short- or medium-term investments like those offered by the banks, building societies and National Savings – when time is very short, it would be foolish to put any money into an investment where you run the risk of receiving back less than you pay in. Look for low-risk, flexible investments and shop around for those with the best returns.

Pre-retirement, therefore, ought to be the period when we adjust our existing financial plans for a smooth and comfortable retirement, but for most people it is the time when they first begin to realise just how important financial planning is. As long as the penny drops in time, action can still be taken to sort out financial problems. But the important thing to remember is that the sooner you act the better – any delay can be very costly in terms of reduced retirement benefits.

Summary

1. Do you have term insurance which you could safely allow to lapse?
2. Are you taking full advantage of the contribution limits on your pension?
3. Should your investment strategy become more cautious?
4. Are you making full use of the available 'tax-free' investments?

19 Retirement

This is the point at which you should be able to sit back and enjoy the fruits of a lifetime of labour. If you have made reasonable pension provision, and been able, regularly, to put aside a little more money on a long-term basis, you should be able to harvest your personal fortune. This big lump sum can then be invested to produce an income for retirement.

If your financial planning has gone well, your personal wealth should be sufficient to produce a comfortable income to live on. But because no one knows how long they will live for, at this point it is important to remember that over the long term you will require an increasing income to combat the effects of inflation. In the long run, therefore, it is wiser to accept a lower initial percentage yield with prospects for income growth, rather than an initially high yield but with no growth prospects. If you live for, say, a further 20 years after retirement (an increasingly likely prospect), the second scenario means risking not having enough to live on because inflation will probably have eroded your income to a pittance. In financial planning terms you would be 'living too long'! So bearing in mind the effects of inflation, there are various things to consider when your policies mature on retirement.

TAKING PENSION BENEFITS

There is a range of choices available when you come to take your pension benefits. With some occupational, and also personal pension schemes, you can take a smaller pension for the rest of your life and in return, after your death, your widower or widow can receive a higher pension for the remainder of his or her life.

Another option with both occupational and personal pensions is to take part of the pension benefits as a tax-free cash sum to spend as you wish. If you do this, remember that your pension will be reduced. Some company schemes review pensions in payment and, from time to time, make increases to offset the effects of inflation. If your company scheme does not do this, you should consider investing your cash sum to provide an increasing income for the years ahead.

With a personal pension plan, your pension will depend on the prevailing annuity rates and the value of your pension fund. Most plans have an 'open market option' which allows you to shop around for the best rates. The income that you choose can either be fixed or escalating; the latter starts at a lower initial level but increases over the years. Some plans comprise a cluster of separate arrangements, which means you can take just some of your benefits at any particular time. Because you do not have to take all the benefits at once, you are able to 'phase-in' your retirement and have a mixture, or balance of escalating and fixed annuities.

LIFE ASSURANCE AND OTHER SAVINGS PLANS

Before cashing in all your life insurance policies, it might be a good idea to reconsider whether you need life assurance or not. Some whole life policies can go on providing increasing life cover without any more premiums being paid. You may also want to take advice from an insurance adviser about how insurance policies can be used in inheritance tax planning.

If you are fortunate, you may have several policies or savings plans which mature at retirement, producing handsome lump sums: most people spend some of the cash, but very few spend it all at once. These are sums of money that many people have never experienced before, and advice on lump-sum investments may well be helpful. Probably the best place to go for such advice is to a stockbroker. Contrary to popular belief, you do not need vast amounts of money available for investment before you can be accepted by a broker. Many of the provincial firms based outside London are willing to deal with quite small sums and some stockbrokers do not specify a minimum amount. You will receive impartial advice and your investments can be tailored to your individual needs. To find a broker, phone the International Stock Exchange in London and ask them to send a list of stockbrokers in your area.

Some people take up investment as a hobby in their retirement, and you will find many excellent books on lump-sum investment in your local library or book shop. Interesting free publications are also available from the International Stock Exchange, the Unit Trust Association and the Investment Trust Association.

Summary

1. How do you intend to take your pension benefits?
2. Do you still require life insurance for protection?
3. Have you considered planning for inheritance tax? If this worries you why not take advice?
4. How do you want to use any surplus capital? What plans have you made and how will you get the best out of your savings?
5. Have you considered taking impartial financial advice?

CONCLUSION

It should be clear from reading this book that it is not easy to accumulate large sums of money: if it was we could all retire wealthy. But this does not mean we should not at least try. Books on lump-sum investments are limited to helping those who already have money surplus to their requirements, whereas my aim has been to help the saver of any size, from the high-rate taxpayer to the very poor, with some pointers to becoming better off. Whether you end up with a big or a small fortune depends on your circumstances, and your resources, but you will not have any sort of fortune if you do not plan it, so the sooner you start the better.

There are some major hurdles in the way of becoming a successful regular saver. It is, in fact, possible for someone living on the poverty line to be a more successful saver than someone earning £20,000 a year. The key to the whole thing is to cultivate a positive attitude: being cynical and negative and rejecting the idea of saving small sums of money as futile is clearly not the right starting point. Only someone with a positive attitude will be able to take advantage of opportunities as they arise and turn pennies into pounds.

In Part II, we examined the types of savings and investment products available to help you build your wealth. The last hurdle to overcome is to use this knowledge effectively by formulating a personal financial plan. The plan should be based on a frank examination of your own circumstances and asking yourself the right questions. The answers to these questions will help you decide what your needs really are and how to invest your hard-earned money.

I know some people will question the rationale of this book: 'What is the point of planning your fortune? Aren't you only saving for savings sake? You can't take it with you when you die.' The answer, as I have tried to emphasise, is that you really do need a small fortune in order to produce the income on which to retire comfortably. The state is under no obligation to maintain your standard of living at the pre-retirement level, let alone to provide you with enough money to buy champagne, caviar or holidays in sunny Spain. If your retirement is going to be one long happy holiday it is going to cost you a fortune, and it will take a lot of planning. So don't just sit there – do something about it before it is too late!

Index